A Civil War Journey:
The Letters of John W. Brendel
11th Pennsylvania Volunteer Infantry Regiment

Justin T. Mayhue

Copyright 2006
All rights reserved
Printed in the United States of America

Second printing

Printing:
Copyquik Printing & Graphics
710 Oak Hill Avenue
Hagerstown, Maryland 21740

ISBN 978-0-9790983-0-7

For additional information, you may contact the editor

Justin T. Mayhue
13726 Paradise Church Road
Hagerstown, Maryland 21742
301-791-2449

Symbols for maps and photographs
AC - American Civil War.com
LOC - Library of Congress
NA - National Archives
NPS - National Park Service

Front Cover- *Soldiers at rest after drill, Petersburg, Virginia.* NA
*The Editor's research indicates that this is most likely
the photograph of John W. Brendel.*

Acknowledgements

It is with humble gratitude that I recognize the following individuals and organizations for contributing to the success of this book:

- To my wife Diana and children - Lisa & Philip: Thanks for your patience and encouragement. Lisa transcribed many of the letters onto the computer.

- Historian Ted Alexander reviewed content and provided encouragement.

- Michael Weller provided editorial expertise.

- Ed Hahn and the staff at the Westmoreland Historical Society provided valuable information on Brendel's family history.

- John Frye & Marsha Fuller of the Washington County Free Library, Western Maryland Room allowed access to books and documents.

- West Newton Cemetery provided cemetery records for the Brendel family.

- Frank Long provided Brendel family geneologly records.

- The staff of Copyquik Printing made this project a reality.

- Special appreciation is extended to Jane Cooper Myers and son Harry Myers for making John W. Brendel's letters available for all to enjoy.

Contents

Introduction 7

Chapter 1 (1862- The Journey Begins) 11

Chapter 2 (1863- On The March) 31

Chapter 3 (1864- May God Bless Us All) 85

Chapter 4 (1865- Rebs Are Deserting) 145

Appendix A 167

Appendix B 170

End Notes 173

Bibliography 179

Index 183

About the Editor 191

VOLUNTEER ENLISTMENT.

STATE OF *Pennsylvania* **TOWN OF** *Coal Valley*

I, *John W. Brendel* born in *Westmoreland* in the State of *Pennsylvania* aged *37* years, and by occupation a *Shoemaker* DO HEREBY ACKNOWLEDGE to have volunteered this *Thirteenth* day of *August* 1864 to serve as a **Soldier** in the Army of the United States of America, for the period of *THREE YEARS*, unless sooner discharged by proper authority: Do also agree to accept such bounty, pay, rations, and clothing, as are, or may be, established by law for volunteers. And I, *John Brendle* do solemnly swear, that I will bear true faith and allegiance to the **United States of America**, and that I will serve them honestly and faithfully against all their enemies or opposers whomsoever; and that I will observe and obey the orders of the President of the United States, and the orders of the officers appointed over me, according to the Rules and Articles of War.

Sworn and subscribed to, at *Pittsburgh* this *13th* day of *August* 18*64*   *John W Brendel*
BEFORE *A. S. Nicholson — all*

I CERTIFY, ON HONOR, That I have carefully examined the above named Volunteer, agreeably to the General Regulations of the Army, and that in my opinion he is free from all bodily defects and mental infirmity, which would, in any way, disqualify him from performing the duties of a soldier.

EXAMINING SURGEON.

I CERTIFY, ON HONOR, That I have minutely inspected the Volunteer, previously to his enlistment, and that he was entirely sober when enlisted; that, to the best of my judgment and belief, he is of lawful age; and that, in accepting him as duly qualified to perform the duties of an able-bodied soldier, I have strictly observed the Regulations which govern the recruiting service. This soldier has *hazel* eyes, *dark* hair, *dark* complexion, is *5* feet *9* inches high.

John B Ulyen

Capt 11th Regiment of *Penna* Volunteers,
Gov. PRINT. OFF. July, 186_   RECRUITING O___

↑ Enlistment document - John W. Brendel's Enlistment Document. NA

Envelope used by Brendel to send one of 144 letters home. →

6

Introduction

The letters of John W. Brendel, a soldier in the 11th Pennsylvania Volunteer Infantry Regiment, allows the reader to get a glimpse inside the mind of a Civil War soldier. Whether your interest in the American Civil War is casual or you are a hardcore student, you will come away with a fresh perspective on the war and life experiences of one soldier during the period of 1862 - 1865, in these previously unpublished letters. Brendel participated in nearly every major engagement of the Army of the Potomac from the Battle of South Mountain through Appomattox (see Appendix B).

Brendel was born August 6, 1825 in Westmoreland County, Pennsylvania. Brendel entered military service at the age of thirty-seven, somewhat old to be a soldier. The typical soldier was white, protestant and single and between the ages of 18 and 29 however, ages of soldiers covered a broad range.[1] The thoughts and ideas conveyed in his letters are that of a mature individual. However, his grammar and punctuation skills are poor. It is the author's intention to keep the main context of the letters in Brendel's own words and thoughts. Editing the letters consisted of correcting some grammar & spelling and most punctuation (periods are missing quite often).

On June 22, 1853, John W. Brendel joined in holy matrimony with Anna M. McLaughlin by Robert Singer, Justice of the Peace at Jones Mills, Westmoreland County, Pennsylvania. By 1862, they had three children, Jenny 8 years old, Sammy 4 years old and Robert (Robbie) 2 years old. Before the war Brendel's occupation was a shoemaker.

Brendel enlisted on August 13, 1862 at Coal Valley, Pennsylvania. At that time, he was 5 feet 9 inches tall, just above the average height of a soldier, dark hair, hazel eyes and a dark complexion. Brendel was recruited by Captain John McGrew of the 11th Pennsylvania

Volunteer Infantry Regiment, Company G. By the end of August, the 11th Pennsylvania was assigned to the First Corps, Second Division, Third Brigade in the Army of the Potomac.[2]

In the letters, Brendel shares his concerns about his health and his family's health. Soldiers were exposed to illness and disease that did not exist at home. The lack of nutritious food and poor sanitary conditions led to far more casualties than bullets from the enemy. This was also the first time that many of these men were away from home for any length of time. The soldiers were exposed to illness and disease for which they had no built up immunity. Illness was not confined only to the army. Illness at home was a major concern for Brendel. Being hundreds of miles from home, he felt helpless when receiving word that a family member was ill. Brendel's wife Anna (maiden name was McLaughlin) was often quite ill.

Anna Brendel wife of John W. Brendel, photo taken during the Civil War

Family members especially wives were required to tend to the family affairs normally conducted by the men. Army regulation required each soldier receive pay every two months. However, receiving pay was haphazard. The soldier may receive a partial payment every couple of months or not be paid at all for up to six months. Bills were piling up at home with no means of paying them. Brendel attempts to send money home via; letters, Adams Express and soldiers returning home.

Homesickness was as much of a concern as the enemy. Soldiers looked forward to mail. It was very discouraging to see other soldiers receiving mail but receiving none for themselves. Brendel is not shy about wanting mail. He argues back and forth with his wife about not receiving enough letters. The mail system was not perfect. Sometimes mail would go to another regiment or would not catch up to a moving army for sometime. It is interesting and sometimes comical how Brendel responds to not receiving letters from home.

Even through the most difficult of times, Brendel's deep faith in God enabled him to believe that he would survive. Brendel mentions his religious convictions and beliefs throughout the war. "My faith has always been strong enough to believe that I would get home again when I went into battles. I had no fear of being killed. I put my trust in God and I knew he was able to take care of me."

Brendel relays through pen and paper to his wife about numerous other topics including; trading items with the enemy, weather conditions, high prices for food, stamps and tobacco, other soldiers from back home and his politics. As a staunch Democrat, he is not shy about his views of Lincoln and McClellan.

In addition to the letters, the activities of the Army of The Potomac including general military strategies and movements of the 11th Pennsylvania Volunteer Infantry Regiment are included to coincide with the general timeframe of each letter. Also included are definitions and/or explanations about Civil War terms not common in today's language. You will gain a greater appreciation of Brendel's journey and military events if you understand the military's structure. The following information provides a breakdown of the strength of each military component:

Company - *(designated by a letter) - 100 men were authorized*

Regiment - *(basic military unit-designated by a number and name of a state) - 10 companies or about 1,000 men*

Brigade - *(designated by a number) - 3 to 4 Regiments*

Division - *(designated by a number) - 2 to 3 Brigades*

Corps - *(designated by a number or Roman Numeral) - 2 or more Divisions*

The number of soldiers in each unit varied greatly as the war progressed. Seldom did units have the desired number of soldiers. As an example after the Battle of Gettysburg, only eleven men remained in his company.

The study of battles and leaders plays an importance role in our understanding events of the Civil War. The individual soldier sacrificed the most to accomplish military objectives. The study of the Civil War should not be just about numbers. The study of individual soldiers brings the human element of war to the forefront.

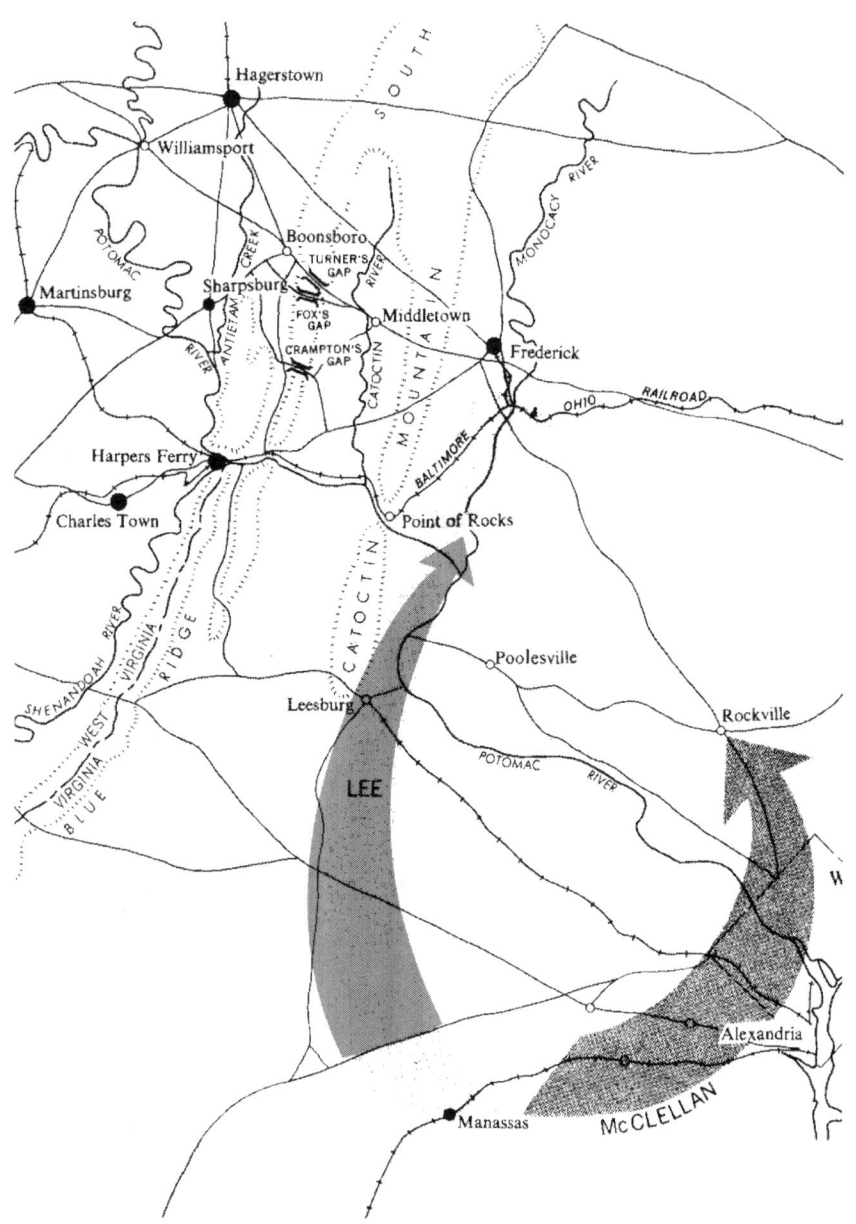

Maryland Campaign Map, September 3-18, 1862 (NPS)

10

Chapter 1

1862 - *The Journey Begins*

John W. Brendel entered the military (mustered-in) as a private at Camp Curtin on August 25, 1862. Camp Curtin was a military training camp near Harrisburg, Pennsylvania. Over 300,000 soldiers passed through Camp Curtin making it the largest Federal camp used during the Civil War. The camp and surrounding area also served as a supply depot, hospital and prisoner of war camp.[1]

The camp was named after Pennsylvania's wartime Governor Andrew Curtin. Governor Curtin rallied support for the Union cause and helped solidify the key role that Pennsylvania played in preserving the Union.[2] Brendel wrote his first letter as a soldier from Camp Curtin.

Written to:
Mrs. Annie M. Brendel
Westnewton, Westmoreland County, Penna.

Camp Curtin
August 30, 62

Dear Wife:

After my love to you and the children, I would like to inform you that I am well at present and hoping these few lines will find you enjoying the summer blessing. Enclosed you will find a receipt for twenty dollars which I sent by Adams Express. Esgr. Weiner is the agent in West Newton. I got ten dollars in Pittsburg [sic] and twenty-nine dollars in Harrisburg and fifteen dollars to get into Washington City. I have fifty dollars to get from Allegheny County. They had paid out all of there funds until they get more. I was in Harrisburg yesterday and got likeness and it was so poor that I will not have it, but as soon as I get a chance I will send you another one. We will leave for the regiment on Wednesday night. As soon as this comes to hand, I would like to know whether you got the receipt or if I don't get an answer from you before we leave, I will write to you when we get to the regiment. Give my respects to all friends. I expect to see the boys next week. Nothing more at present, but remain your affectionate husband until death.

John W. Brendel

You have to take the receipt to the agent or you cannot get the money. I will send you more in a few days. Good by, take good care of yourself until I see you again.

It was not uncommon for soldiers to receive a bounty or a bonus as an incentive to join.

The term "likeness" refers to a photograph or Carde de Visite (small visiting card portrait).

Brendel mentions the Adams Express. Founded in 1840 by Alvin Adams, the company delivered parcels of every size to soldiers. They could be compared to today's version of the United Parcel Service (UPS) or Federal Express. Adams Express became a household name by delivering food clothing or other non-essentials from home.[3] The Adams express company is still in business today as an investment firm.

While Private Brendel was writing his first letter, Union General John Pope's Army of Virginia was engaged in battle with Confederate General Robert E. Lee's Army of Northern Virginia at Bull Run/Manassas, Virginia August 29-30. In the North, battles were typically named after geographical landmarks. Southern battles were named after a town in proximity to the event.

After the defeat at Bull Run, the Union Army pulled back to the defenses of Washington D.C. to reorganize. On September 2, President Lincoln placed General George B. McClellan in charge of all Federal forces around Washington.

On September 3, Lee wrote a letter to Confederate President Jefferson Davis from near Dranesville, Virginia outlining and justifying his immediate plans. "The present seems to be the most propitious time since the commencement of the war for the Confederate army to enter Maryland." Lee felt that the Federal armies were weak and demoralized. "If it is ever desired to give material aid to Maryland and afford her an opportunity of throwing off the oppression to which she is now subject, this would seem the most favorable" Lee said. In the next paragraph Lee states - "The purpose, if discovered, will have the effect of carrying the enemy north of the Potomac."[4] By taking the war beyond the Potomac River, Virginia would be spared the ravages of war, at least for awhile.

Written to:
Mrs. Annie M. Brendel
Westnewton, Westmorland County, Penna.
*Soldiers Letter-Due 3 cents

                                        Washington City
                                          Sept 8, 62

Dear Wife:

I received your kind letter just as we were leaving Harrisburg and was glad to hear from you. I am well, we are about ready to start to the regiment. Sixty of our company was in the last fight (ed. Bull Run) and ten wounded and three killed. Captain Bearer [sic] is wounded and is here, but I did not get to see. The first lieutenant was wounded and has gone home. I do not have time to write at present. I will write as soon as I get to the regiment and give you the particulars. We have twelve miles to where our regiment lies. Nothing more at present but remain your affectionate Husband.

John W. Brendel

Captain Jacob J. Bierer enlisted September 9, 1861 with Company C, 11th Pennsylvania at Latrobe, Westmoreland County. Bierer was wounded at second Bull Run and discharged April 2, 1864.

At Bull Run, in the vicinity of Chinn Ridge more than forty soldiers of the 11th Pennsylvania were killed and another two hundred wounded or missing in action. This regiment suffered more casualties than any other regiment in the fight.[5]

During the Civil War, postage was not required to be pre-paid for soldiers. The words "Soldiers Letter" was written on the envelope. The postage was paid upon delivery.

Written to:
No envelope

Camp near Silver Spring
Sept. 9, 1862

Dear Wife:

Sat down to drop you a few lines to let you know that I am well at present and hope you are enjoying the same blessing. We left Camp Curtin last Saturday morning and got into Baltimore last Saturday evening. Left Baltimore on Sunday and got into Washington City Sunday and left there yesterday and got here yesterday. I went and took supper with William and Lawyer last evening and they are well and look fine. Their company was in the last fight at Bull Run and suffered considerably. Their commissioned officers were all wounded. Our company five killed and thirteen wounded and drove our division back to here. Our loss was heavy. We are expected to get marching orders every hour. There are any amount of people here that I know. Kiss Jenny and baby for me and tell them to be good children. Croft Koontz is here driving. I did not get my sixty-three dollars yet, but when I get it I will send it to you, fifty dollars of it. I am to get a bond on the old Pittsburg Bank, paid the first of January. Nothing more at present but remain your affectionate husband. Write to: Washington City D.C. care of J.B. McGrew Co. G 11th P.V. Colonel Coulter.

The William that Brendel refers to is William McLaughlin. McLaughlin is Brendel's brother-in-law. McLaughlin enlisted on September 9, 1861 in the 11th Pennsylvania Infantry Company C. By the end of the war, McLaughlin attained the rank of captain.

General McClellan's reorganization of the army placed the 11th Pennsylvania in the First Corps, Second Division, Third Brigade.[6] Shortly after writing his letter dated September 9, Brendel and the

11th Pennsylvania would accompany the Union army west in pursuit of the Confederates.

On September 9, Lee divided his army into five segments. General Jackson and three divisions were sent southwest to capture the federal garrisons at Harpers Ferry and Martinsburg, Virginia. General's Lee and Longstreet proceeded to Hagerstown, Maryland. General D.H. Hill's Division remained just east of Boonsboro, Maryland on top of South Mountain to act as a rear guard.[7]

On September 14, Brendel (having only serving for three weeks and with very little formal military training) would see combat for the first time. At 3 a.m. the 11th Pennsylvania awoke to the sound of reveille. By 5 a.m. they were marching towards South Mountain.

Arriving in the vicinity of the battlefield, knapsacks (backpack which held extra clothing and a blanket) were dropped on Old Braddock Road and a battle line was formed. At about 4 p.m., the First Corps moved up the mountain engaging the Confederates who were protecting the mountain passes just north of the National Road at Turners Gap.

It was a tough struggle fighting over treacherous terrain. The Confederates were inferior in numbers but held the advantage of occupying the higher ground. At about dark, Brig. General George Gordon Meade's Third Division pressed the Confederates (under the command of Brig. General Robert Rodes) over the crest of South Mountain. Throughout the day, Union forces fought for two other mountain passages south of Turners Gap: Fox's and Crampton's Gaps. The Confederates retreated during the night of the 14th concentrating their forces in the area of Sharpsburg, Maryland.

After receiving a fresh supply of hard bread (hardtack) on the morning of the 15th, the Union army advanced over South Mountain. Hardtack was a staple for the army consisting of a three-inch square baked cracker made of flour and water. Hardtack often was very hard and/or laden with insects. The cracker was filling, but contained very little nutritional value.

On the night of the 15th, the 11th Pennsylvania camped along Antietam Creek, one mile from Keedysville, Maryland.

On the afternoon of the 16th, the 11th Pennsylvania crossed Antietam Creek proceeding in the direction of Sharpsburg. The 11th Pennsylvania, under the First Corps command of General Hooker, was assigned the right flank of the army. The regiment spent the night in a cornfield, near Smoketown Road.[8]

On the morning of September 17, 1862, the Battle of Antietam commenced. The 11th Pennsylvania formed in line of battle with other regiments of the Third Brigade. The Brigade was comprised of members from the 12th and 13th Massachusetts and 83rd New York under the command of General Hartsuff. General Hartsuff was wounded early in the battle and replaced by Colonel Richard Coulter. The Third Brigade advanced to the vicinity of the East Woods and the eastern end of farmer David Miller's cornfield.

According to Coulter, "The advance was maintained under a most severe fire of artillery and infantry, which however, was as briskly replied to as the forward movement would admit of." The brigade went into action at 5 a.m. and retired about 9 a.m. For two hours of that time, it was exposed to the most galling fire.[9]

The enemy in the immediate front was General Harry Hay's "Louisiana Tigers". The Louisianans drove Hartsuff's (Coulters) Brigade to the edge of the East Woods where Union soldiers rallied and stood there ground. According to Lieutenant George P. Ring of the 6th Louisiana Infantry, "We advanced some three hundred and fifty yards and then commenced firing upon the enemy who were in front of a wood about two hundred yards off, protected by a battery. We stood there about half an hour and found ourselves all cut to pieces. They had charged into the cornfield where the lead was flying around like the bees to a hornets nest. Of the 550 men Hays led into battle, 323 were killed or wounded.[10]

The Union's 12th Massachusetts lost 224 of 334 men taken into the cornfield. This sixty-seven percent loss was the highest of any Federal regiment on that day.

At 2 p.m. the division moved to the right near Hagerstown Road in support of artillery batteries. The regiment remained at that location through the 18th. With over 23,000 casualties, the Battle of Antietam would go down in history as the single bloodiest day during the Civil War.

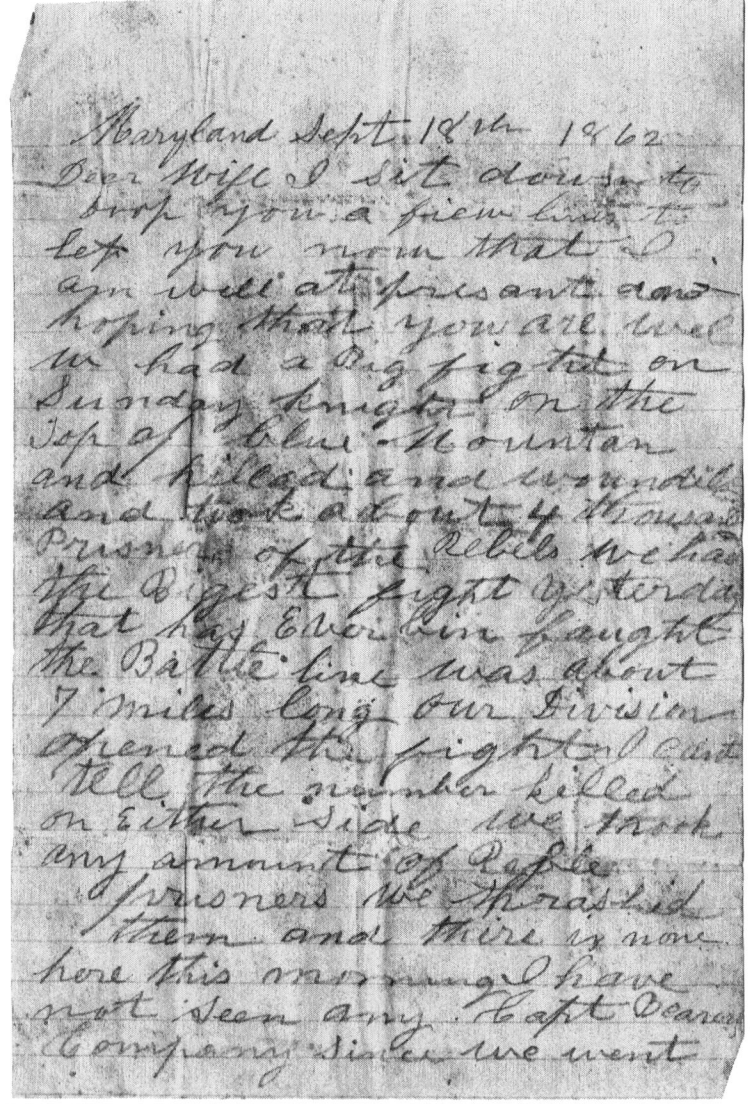

Original letter written by John W. Brendel while still on the battlefield at Antietam.

Written to:
No envelope

Maryland
September 18, 62

Dear Wife,

I sit down to drop you a few lines to let you know that I am well at present and hoping that you are well. We had a big fight on Sunday night on top of Blue Mountain and killed and wounded and took about four thousand prisoners of the Rebels. We had the biggest fight yesterday that has ever been fought. The battle line was about seven miles long our division opened the fight. I can't tell the number killed on either side we took any amount of Rebel prisoners. We thrashed them and there is none here this morning. I have not seen any of Captain Bearor's [sic] company since we went into the fight. Will is along with wagon train. I have not got my money yet that bond on the Pittsburg bank has not come yet but the Captain says he will attend to it. Well Ann, I saw the elephant (ed. experienced war) twice, on Blue Mountain and here. This is about two miles from the Potomac River. I will give you the particulars in the next. We was laying down and a shell struck left-hand man and knocked the side of his head off. It almost raised me off the ground. Well Ann, this is Rebel paper, my paper is on Blue Mountain. I must stop my paper is all. Your husband till death,

John W. Brendel

The Blue Mountain Brendel is referring to is known today as South Mountain.

As soon as the firing ceased, details were sent out to bury the dead. At Antietam the 11th Pennsylvania lost an officer and twenty-six men. Additionally, four officers and eighty-five men were wounded. Two soldiers were taken prisoner.

On the night of September 18th, the Rebels retreated back to Virginia. A majority of the Union forces remained between Sharpsburg and Harpers Ferry until November.[11]

Written to:
Mrs. J. W. Brendel
West Newton, Pa.

Washington Co. Md.
Sept.21

Dear Ann:

I received your letter this morning. The first since I left Camp Curtin. I was glad to here from you that you were all well. I have not been very well for four days. Last Sunday I was in the fight on Blue Mountain and in this battle last week and it was the biggest ever fought. General McClellan was here himself. William and Lawyer both are well. I have better than Seventy-six dollars coming to me. As soon as I get it, I will send it to you. I wrote you a letter day before yesterday. Excuse me for not writing more. Direct your letters as usual to Washington City. The mail follows us wherever we go. We have been moving every day nearly. Give my respects to all inquiring friends. I received a letter from Jane. Write to her and tell her the boys are well. Nothing more at present, but remaining your loving husband until death,

John W. Brendel

Write soon, here is a Rebel postage stamp. I got a good Rebel blanket and testament. I would like to send the testament to Jenny if I had the chance, but I will try to bring it along when I come.

Written to:
Mrs. Anna M. Brendel
West Newton, Westmorland Co. Pa.

                              Camp near Sharpsburg
                              October the 1st 1862

Dear Wife:

I received your letter last evening and was glad to here from you, but was sorry to hear that you were not well. I have not been well myself since the South Mountain fight. I got cold that night. We have not moved from here since the fight, the last on the 17th. I want you to let me know if you have any money yet, and how you are getting along. I expect we will get some money in a few days. I have only received two letters from you since I left Harrisburg. Write as soon as this comes to hand. I don't want you to be scrubbing peoples old houses. I think I can make money enough to keep you and the children if I keep my health. Tell Jenny that I will write her a letter as soon as I get the time. I was on guard last night and today. Give my love to the children and keep a good portion for yourself. Direct letters as usual. Nothing more at present, but remain your affectionate husband,

John W. Brendel

On October 3, the brigade was reviewed by President Lincoln, Generals McClellan and Reynold's. In addition to reviewing the soldiers, President Lincoln visited the battlefields of South Mountain and Antietam.

On October 26, the division moved through Crampton's Gap, crossing the Potomac River on a pontoon bridge at Berlin (Brunswick) Maryland. A pontoon bridge is constructed of wooden planks tied together over small boats or pontoons. Men, horses and wagons can cross a well constructed bridge. The division moved through Lovettsville, Virginia en route to the vicinity of Warrenton, Virginia.[12]

Written to:
No envelope

Virginia
November 2, 1862

Dear Wife:

I received two letters last Saturday a week ago and was very glad to hear from you that you were all well. We got marching orders Sunday morning and I had not time to write to you until now. I expect we will stay here until tomorrow. We crossed the Potomac River nine miles below Harpers Ferry at Berlin (ed. Brunswick) on a pontoon bridge. The Rebels burned the bridge when we routed them from Antietam. There was some heavy cannonading. We are on the Winchester Turnpike. Dear Ann I have been very un-well since the South Mountain fight. The citizens call it the Blue Mountain. We got shelter tents (ed. small canvas tarps) last Thursday. We had none till then. We have plenty of clothing. I have two good blankets. I commenced taking medicine yesterday for the first time, but I have been to my post every day. We were mustered for our pay, day before yesterday and I think we will get it in ten or twelve days. I will send you my wages as soon as I get it. Tell Plummer that he shall have his rent as soon as the government pays off. You must excuse me for not writing you a better letter my head is not in order to write. This is an old sheet of paper I had in my pocket. We have twelve-thousand men in our division. I must quit, nothing more at present, bur remain your affectionate husband,

John W. Brendel

Write soon

On November 7, General McClellan was relieved of command by President Lincoln. Maj. General Ambrose Burnside replaced McClellan as commanding General of the Army. President Lincoln felt General McClellan was too slow in pursuing the Confederates.[13]

On November 8, the brigade moved to support cavalry General George Bayard.[14] Bayard would be mortally wounded at the battle of Fredericksburg December 13, 1862 along the Rappahannock river.[15] The enemy was on the opposite bank of the river during the exchange.

Written to:
No envelope

Warrington, Va.
Nov. 8, 1862

Dear Wife:

I sit down this morning to drop you a few lines to let you know that I am pretty well at present and hope you are enjoying the same blessings. We got here yesterday and it snowed all day. It is pleasant this morning. This is the first snow we had this fall. There was about four thousand Rebels here but they all left without a fight. See Ann you must get along as well as you can till I get my money. I will send you it as soon as we draw it. I expect we will get it in a few days. Write as soon as this comes to hand. I will write as soon as we get to some stopping place. Give my respects to all inquiring friends. Nothing more at present, but remain your loving husband until death,

John W. Brendel

I thought I would drop you these few lines to let you know where I am.

General Burnside's plan was to concentrate Union forces at Falmouth, Virginia. He then planned to cross the river and engage the Confederates in Fredericksburg.[16]

Written to:
Mrs. Ann M. Brendel
West Newton, Westmorland County, Penna.

Camp 11th Regt. Liberty,
Bealeton Station Virg.
November the 21st. 1862

Dear wife:

I sit down with a sorrowful heart tonight to drop you a few lines to let you know that I received your letter of the 18th and to here of you being sick, but my dear wife you must put your trust in God and he will take care of you if you put your trust in him. Dear Annie you said you are afraid we will never meet on earth again. But my wife I believe we will for I trust in God and I believe with all my heart that he will permit us to meet on earth again. You must not get down hearted but cheer up and pray to God with your whole heart and mind that we will meet on earth and I believe we will for God has promised whatsoever we ask in faith we shall receive and God won't lie. My love I must tell you something about what a time we had today, the Johnny Rebs as we call them and sometimes we call them gray backs made a dash on our picket line and captured five of our fellows but I think they were all conscripts (ed. drafted) for you ought to just been here to see them get up and dust themselves when they saw us old veterans come. You would've laughed to see them get. My dear wife you must get Lighty or somebody, Elie to write to me as quick as this comes to hand if you are not better I will go to General Meade and try and get a furlough and come home. I will have to show him the letter you sent me if I want to get a furlough. They hardly ever give any till we get into winter quarters and I hope that will be before long. It commenced raining today and has rained all day slow and steady and is raining now it is just 9 o'clock. How I would like to be at home now talking to you in place of fighting but thank God we can talk through pen and paper while other poor fellows have to get somebody to write for them. We have very hard picket duty to do here. We are on picket every other day. I will be on picket tomorrow if God spares my life and health. I just feel middling I was sick some *few days ago I just weighed 127lbs. One year ago I weighed 180lbs. My dear wife, enclosed you will find five dollars. I would send you more but as soon as I can get a chance I will send you more. Give my love to my dear little children and tell them they have a pap that loves them. Tell them to be good children till pap comes home and I hope that will be before long. Give my respects to all inquiring friends. My love to you my dear wife with my whole heart and trust to God. We will soon meet I'm not so weak in faith as you for I believe God will permit us to meet again. Will is well and lawyer is still away from the regiment yet but is still getting better. He is able to get about himself right as soon as this comes to hand for I am so anxious to hear from you I don't expect I will sleep much till I hear from you for I don't sleep much at night anyhow. If you are no better get somebody to write and I will try hard to get home. May God protect us through life and at last receive us all in Heaven. Your affectionate husband,*

John W. Brendel

Pickets were guards usually consisting of forty to fifty men posted in a line ahead of the main army force. If attacked, pickets would warn the main force thus preventing a surprise attack.

Both North and South were forced to initiate a conscription (draft). The Confederate draft law went into effect in April 1862. The Union draft law went into effect in March 1863. The quality of drafted men was often much less than patriotic volunteer soldiers.[17]

Written to:
Anne M. Brendel
West Newton, Westmorland County Penna.

> Camp, Aquia Creek Landing
> November 26, 1862

Dear Wife,

After my love to you I would inform you that I received a letter from you and was very glad to hear from you that you was all well. I had now a chance to write to you since I have to write whenever I can get a chance. We have had two snow storms this fall since we have been marching and several rains it rained all last night but there is three of us in a mess (ed. tent) and we sleep very comfortable. We have had plenty to eat till a few days ago and we bought six pounds of flour and baked shortcake and it went good to us. You will have to shift the best you can till I get my money. You said you was going to buy a hog if you can it would be a very good idea. I have five cents yet and tried to get a stamp but could not get it so I have to send it without paying the postage. I loaned the captain three dollars and he took sick and has not been with us since we left Sharpsburg MD. He has not lifted my bond on Allegheny County or you could get it cashed. He was to have had it fixed before we left Harrisburg nor did I get the months wages in advance. I had a notion to get somebody in West Newton to attend to it is fifty dollars the bond. Dear Anny you said you was afraid I would run off with some of the girls. You need not be afraid for we don't get to see many of them. I forgot to tell you of my health it has not been good since the battle at South Mountain. I have been taking medicine for about three weeks and have lost 40 lbs in weight so you can tell whether I feel very good. We are sixty miles from Richmond we are four miles from the landing where we can take the gunboat for Richmond. Nothing more at present but want you to write often for it is the pleasure I have to hear from you. Soldier's life is a hard life to live. Your loving husband give my love to Jenny and Robby and kiss them for me,

John W. Brendel

Write soon and often if you love me. Excuse scribbling and mistakes.

Aquia Creek landing is located northeast of Fredericksburg along the banks of the Potomac River.

Written to:
Anne M. Brown
West Newton, Westmorland County Penna.

Camp near Aquia Creek
December 8, 1862

Dear Wife,

After my love to you I would inform you that I wrote you a letter more then a week ago and got no answer from you yet and I think it very long to hear from you. I am not well yet we have been at Aquia Creek for several days unloading vessels and loading cars. We left there last Friday evening and marched seven miles towards Belle Plains. We are going to march there tomorrow. It snowed all day Friday we got into camp about 10 o'clock at night and the snow was about four or five inches deep. We scraped the snow off the ground and struck our tents and made our fire. Made a cup of coffee and went to bed and lay very comfortable till morning and it has been hard freezing since. I got part of my money last Saturday I got thirty-two dollars and ninety-three cents I will have twenty-six dollars more coming to me the first of the month. Enclosed you will find two dollars we are afraid to send money from here for fear of losing it. I will send you my money as soon as we get to some place where I can send it with safety. If you need any money maybe you can borrow some till I send mine home that will be in a day or two I expect. I can send if from Belle Plains that is four or five miles from here. I did not pay the postage on the last letter. I could not get a stamp. Nothing more at present but remain your loving husband until death,

J. W. Brendel

It has cost me eight dollars for tobacco since I left home. Write soon for it seems long to hear from you.

On December 13, the 11th Pennsylvania fought at the Battle of Fredericksburg. Assigned to the left wing of the army, they advanced against General Thomas (Stonewall) Jackson's Corps. Casualties suffered by The Army of the Potomac included: 1,284 killed, 9,600 wounded and 1,769 captured or missing.[18]

Written to:
Mrs. Anne M. Brendel
West Newton, Westmorland County Penna.

Christmas
December 25, 1862

Dear Anny,

I have received your kind letter and was very glad to hear from you that you was all well I feel a little better today. I sent you five dollars and fifty cents to Jenny and Robby before I received this letter from you and I gave Captain McGrew fifteen dollars more today. His wife is to send it to you immediately. She will either bring it to you or send it by one of his boys. We are encamped near Belle Plains we may probably stay here till spring. There is a strong talk of our regiment going to Washington City. I don't know for sure whether it would go for sure I wish it would. We have got our little houses fixed up pretty warm. The size of ours is 6ft x 7ft for three of us. You wanted to know about renting the house Plummer told me I could have the house till I come home if I wanted it and wrote to me too. So you can do as you please about it. I feel weak and tired I would like to write more to you but my head is so dizzy. I can't keep my mind together to write. You will have to excuse me I want you to write as soon as this comes to hand. Send me some postage stamps they are scarce here. Nothing more at present, your loving husband,

John W. Brendel

Inclement weather such as heavy rain or snow often made roads impassable. Severe cold also adversely affected personnel. When armies were hampered by untenable conditions winter quarters were established. These camps often resembled small cities. Tents were laid out in neat rows with streets in between. Sometimes streets were givin names.

Idle time was spent by reading newspapers or periodicals. Two favorites, founded in 1857, were *The Atlantic Monthly* and *Harpers Weekly*. Soldiers played card games, checkers, poker and even the dice game called "Chuck-or Luck". Other Games included; baseball, wrestling, cockfights, boxing and blanket tossing.[19]

Some regiments had mascots or pets that accompanied them into battle. The 11th Pennsylvania had a bull terrier named "Sallie". Sallie began her tenure with the regiment at Camp Wayne near West Chester, Pennsylvania. She went to battle staying with the regiment as shot and shell was whizzing all around.

At Gettysburg, Sallie became separated from the regiment. She was found five days later at the site of the regiment's first day battle (Oak Ridge) licking wounds and standing vigil over the dead. She would not leave the field until all the soldiers were removed.

Sallie was struck down by a Confederate's bullet at the Battle of Hatchers Run, Virginia on February 6, 1865. She was honored for her dedication by the regiment at Gettysburg. The 11th Pennsylvania monument includes a bronze sculpture of Sallie at the base.[20]

Other regiments went to war with more unusual mascots. The 8th Wisconsin Infantry had an eagle named "Old Abe" and the 12th Wisconsin Infantry had a bear.[21]

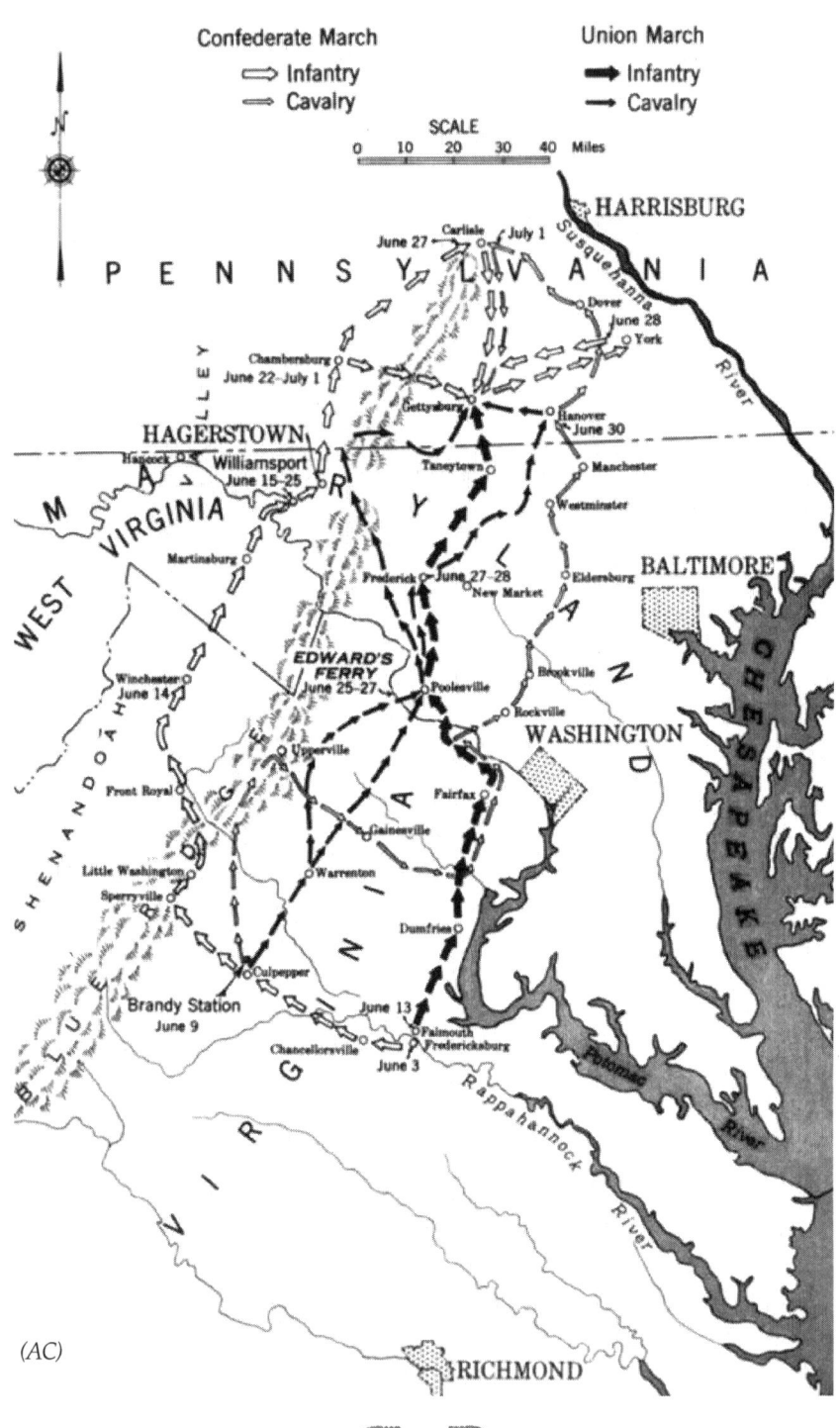

Chapter 2

1863 - On The March

On September 22, 1862, President Lincoln issued the preliminary Emancipation Proclamation. Lincoln waited for a Union victory before issuing the proclamation. It says in part: "On the first day of January, in the year of our Lord one thousand eight hundred sixty-three, all persons held as slaves within any State, or designated part of a state the people whereof shall then be in rebellion against the United States, shall be then, thenceforward, forever free." The perceived victory at Antietam became the mechanism.[1]

It is unclear how much information Brendel knew about the war aims. On his mind was family, health and finances.

On January 2, all arms of .57 caliber and .58 caliber in the 11th Pennsylvania were replaced with .69 caliber rifled muskets.[2]

Written to:
No envelope

Camp near Bell Landing, Virginia
January the 3rd

Dear Ann:

I received your letter last evening and was glad to here from you that you was all well but I was sorry to hear that Jenny was not well. I am better I am on duty today. You wanted to know what a corporal was. A corporal is a non-commissioned officer. I am in the same company and regiment. You wanted my opinion about getting the children baptized. You know my opinion on that without asking it. So you can do as you please about it. It is very cold here too. It snowed here this morning but is clear and windy this afternoon. I am on guard duty today and have not much time to write to you today. As soon as you answer them other letters I wrote to you, I will write again. I sent you a paper yesterday just before I got your letter with a few lines in it. Nothing more at present but kiss the children all for me and give my love to them and keep a good portion for yourself. Give my respects to all inquiring friends, your husband,

John W. Brendel

Corporals assisted Sergeants with organizing the privates during marches, combat and daily camp activities. Brendel was appointed to corporal on November 1, 1862.

Written to:
No envelope

Camp near Bell Plain Landing
January the 14th 1863

Dear Anny:

I sit down once more tonight to write to you to let you know that I feel a great deal better than I was when I last wrote to you. I was very glad to hear from you that you was all well. I received a letter dated the 30th of last month and last year. That seems along time. No letter dated this year yet from you and me charging you so particular in my last two letters to write to me as soon as mine comes to hand. I wanted you to let me know if you got all of the money I sent you. I sent one letter with two dollars and one with five dollars and fifty cents for Jenny and Bobby and I gave Captain McGrew fifteen dollars and Mrs. McGrew was to hand it over immediately to you and this is the reason I wanted to know so particular if you had got it. I would have written sooner to you but was looking every mail to get a letter from you. I received your likeness it looks very natural, but I would sooner been home to seen you yourself. You still keep asking me to send you my likeness. I can't get no likeness taken here. I got one taken in Harrisburg and it was not fit to send. It was blacker than a Negro and left Harrisburg on Saturday morning and landed in Baltimore on Saturday evening and Sunday in Washington City and Monday we went to the regiment. So you see I had no chance to get it taken but I think I will get home pretty soon and you will have the natural likeness and that will be the best. The Captain has got well he is back with us now. I jogged him up about my fifty dollars on Allegheny County and he says he will have it fixed for me immediately. It was due the first of this month. He guaranteed the payment himself or I would have had the money myself before I left Pittsburg and I want to get it in some kind of shape and want you to get somebody to collect it. I must quit the paper is full. Everything is very high. Can't give you nothing more at present but remain your loving husband. But don't take them fretting spells any more.

Take them cool like your husband dose in the battlefield. The ball are flying by the thousands. Answer soon.

J.W. Brendel

The methodology of choice for photography in 1863 was the glass/wet plate method. Using a single glass plate, photograph negatives could be reproduced on paper. Photographs were sent home by soldiers and/or received by family members.[3] Glass plate technology also brought the images of war to civilians who had never witnessed the horrors of a battlefield.[4]

Written to:
No envelope

Camp near Bell Plain Landing
January 18th, 1863

Dear Anny:

I received your kind letter dated January 25 and was very glad to hear from you all. That you was all well. Well I was very sick last night but feel pretty well this Sunday evening. Your letter was miscarried and went to the 11th Cavalry and that detained it a week or two. Captain McGrew got a letter from his wife and she said she would attend to send that money to you immediately and I expect you have got it before this writing and let me know if you have got it or not and I will make it come pretty soon. We are under marching orders now. I expect I will leave here tomorrow or the next day. We can't tell when. I have been jogging the captain up about the bond money and he says he has wrote on about it and he will get it for me. It was due the first of January. If I had known there would been so much fooling around about it I would have had it before I left Pittsburg. I must give you an idea of what we have to pay for things here. When we buy tobacco two dollars per pound and butter I paid one dollar per pound and one dollar for a small chicken and as high as one dollar for a pound of cheese and sixty-two and one-half cents for half pint of honey and seventy-five cents for a can of sauerkraut cooked, ten cents apiece for apples and five cents for little ginger cakes like we get at home. While I have been sick I have to pay this myself. Get nothing but sea biscuit in the bread line and being sick a body gets very tired of such bread. We draw salt pork or fresh beef every day and occasionally rice. We have drawn potatoes twice since we have been here and about a gill of whiskey (ed. four ounces) once since we have been here. Molasses, beans and one onion occasionally. The _____ sons have to pay twenty dollars a barrel for wheat flour and ten for corn. Write as soon as this comes to hand and send me some postage stamps if you have the money to spare for we cannot buy them at all here. I saw them pay as much as ten cents a piece for stamps. So good night and I will come home as soon as I can. I would like very much to see you all tonight. Tell me if J. Boyd went to war or not. Kiss Jenny and baby for me and tell them to be good children till I come home. You did not know that I was appointed corporal about two and one-half months. But remain your affectionate husband,

John W. Brendel

I forgot to tell you the boys are well but would like to be at home. I forget sometimes to tell about them but you can take it for granted they are all right or I mention it.

General stores (sutlers) sprang up in areas where the army was present. These stores sold food and personal items to soldiers at outrageous prices.

On January 20, General Burnside initiated an offensive against the Confederates by moving the army northwest along the Rappahannock River with the intention of crossing at the U.S. Ford. The Union army would strike the left flank of the Confederates.

By nightfall, a steady relentless rain fell, and would not stop for days. The wagons sunk to their hubs. The artillery sank until only the muzzles were out of the mud. Burnside had no choice but to call off the march.

On January 22, the army returned to camp near Falmouth. This debacle would be come known as the "Mud March".[5]

On January 26, President Lincoln replaced Burnside with Joseph Hooker. General Hooker was the First Corps commander who opened the attack at the Battle of Antietam.[6]

Written to:
No envelope

Camp near Bell Landing
January 27th 1863 Virginia

Dear Daughter:

I take my pencil in hand to drop you a few lines from your mother last evening dated the 12th with a postage stamp. It was at the 11th Cavalry in place of the 11th Volunteers. There is a great many letters go wrong, that's the reason they don't get here in time. Jenny, I am not very well, I am not bed fast but I have not done any duty this past march. Jenny I sat down and thought I would write you a nice letter but my head aches so I can not write. You will find a nice little book here that perhaps will do you more good than my writing. You must be a good girl and pray for me till I come to see you. Nothing more at present but give my love to mother and Bobby and kiss them for me. Tell your mother that Lawyer was caught and brought back to the regiment. I wrote to her about it in my last letter. Tell her not to fret herself about him. Your affectionate father,

John W. Brendel

Dear Anny I would write to you but my head is not in order. Write to me as soon as this comes to hand and tell me all about things in general. Tell me if Frithman ever paid that money to you. I think we will be paid off in a few days. They say our paymaster is started out to pay his regiment. Nothing more at present but remain your sincere loving husband,

John W. Brendel

Brendel's daughter Jenny was about eight years old and Bobby (Robert) was two years old when the previous letter was written.

Written to:
Mrs. Ann M. Brendel
West Newton, Westmoreland Co. Pa.

> *Camp near Bell Landing, Virginia*
> *January the 29th 1863*

Dear Wife:

After my love to you I would inform you that I don't feel much better yet, But I hope these lines my find you and family in good health. We had quite a snowstorm here. It commenced raining day before yesterday and yesterday morning it turned to snowing and the snow was about eighteen inches deep. It is pleasant today. I wrote two letters to you since I received yours and I will write as soon as I get an answer from you. Enclosed you will find the documents for to lift my bond on Allegheny County. You said Lighty would attend to it and he has the power of attorney. He can lift the bond and go to the bank and get the money and give it to you and he can keep as much out of it as will pay him for his trouble. He need not let on but what I am a resident of Allegheny County. Tell him to attend to this as soon as possible. The talk is that we will be paid off in a few days. I am mustered in for two months pay but there is three months coming. Write as soon as this comes to hand. Nothing more at present but remain your affectionate husband,

John W. Brendel

Written To:
No envelope

Camp near Bell Landing, Virginia
January the 31st, 1863

Dear Ann:

I received your kind letter last evening dated the 26th. I was very glad to here from you that you was all well. I feel a little better today. I have not much to write to you today. I don't feel like writing today. You said in your letter you would like if I would like to come too. But, I cannot come now but I expect to come before long if God spares my life. You said in one of your letters that Lighty would attend to lifting my bond money on Allegheny County. I sent the papers to you and gave him the power of attorney to lift the money and give it to you. Tell Lighty to never let on but what I am a citizen of Allegheny County. You must excuse me for not writing more to you. I cannot keep my mind together. I received them letters, likeness and stamps and wrote you four or five letters since. Nothing more at present but remain your husband in love,

John W. Brendel

Tell Lighty about that never letting but what I am a citizen of Allegheny. Tell him immediately. Write as soon as this comes to hand. My love to you and the children. I wrote Jenny a letter. If you have not wrote to them at home about Lawyer don't, for they don't know anything about it. The boys are well, so good by. I sent those papers to you day before yesterday the 28th day of January.

Written to:
Mrs. Ann M. Brendel
Westnewton, Westmoreland Co. Penna.

Camp near Bell Landing, Virginia
February 10th, 1863

Dear Ann:

I take my pen in hand to let you know that I received your kind letter today and was very glad to hear from you and that you was well, but I am not well yet. I have the rheumatism. I am better of the diarrhea. If I don't get better soon I will apply for a discharge. Discharges is hard to get now. It was very pleasant here yesterday and today. We have had some very cold rough weather here this winter. I don't think the army can move from here much until spring. We got soft bread today. The first we got since we left Washington. We are to draw three days rations of soft bread a week and two of potatoes and onions. You must be stronger in faith than you are. My faith has always been strong enough to believe that I would get home again. When I went into the battles I had no fear of being killed. I put my trust in God and I knew he would be able to take care of me. You must excuse me for not writing you a better letter. My head is not in order for writing. Frank Reed (ed. probably Francis Reed mustered in July 21, 1862 wounded at Gettysburg: died at Washington, May 22, 1864) sends Jenny a valentine that his lover sent to him. He is a messmate of mine. He often heard me talk of Jenny. I don't think we will get our money till the first of next month. I will have four months wages coming to me then. The boys is well. You need not fret about Lawyer, they won't do much with him. He has not had his trial yet. If you have not wrote to your mother about him you better not say anything to her about it for she will just fret about him. Nothing more at present but remain your loving husband.

John W. Brendel

I got one stamp. Write as soon as this comes to hand. I will send you some money as soon as they pay off.

(poem enclosed titled "The Child and the Butterfly")

*I'm not made for idle play
Like the butterfly all day,
Shameful would it be to grow
Like a dunce, and nothing know:
I must learn to read and look
Often in God's holy book.*

*Busy I must be, and do
What is right and useful too;
What my parents, fond and kind,
Bid me I will gladly mind;*

*Never cause them grief and pain,
Nor will disobey again.
But to God I still will pray,
"Take my wicked heart away;"*

*He from sin can make me free,
For the Saviour died for me.
Oh! How happy life to spend
With the Saviour for my friend*

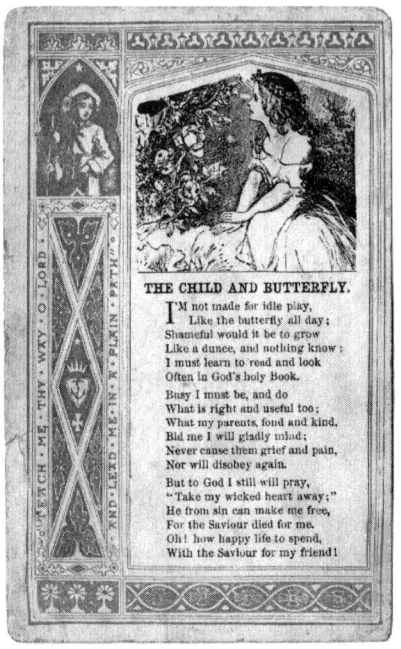

On the back- Presented to Jenny Brendel from a friend

Sickness, poor rations and insufficient medical care became the worst enemies faced by Civil War soldiers. Of over 600,000 fatalities on both sides during the war, about two-thirds (400,000) were the result of disease.[7]

The most prevalent illness was a combination of diarrhea and dysentery. A surgeon noted of hospital admissions: "No matter what else a patient had, he had diarrhea." The condition of loose bowels alone was diarrhea. Loose bowels containing blood was considered dysentery.

Doctors had limited knowledge and drugs available for treatment. One of the major drug therapies was the use of eclectic or plant derived medicine. Treatments included the use of opium; whiskey;

castor oil in the morning and opium at night; calomel (blue mass); turpentine; ipecac and fresh foods.⁽⁸⁾

Written to:
Mrs. Ann M. Brendel
West Newton, Westmorland Co. Penna.

Camp near Bells Landing, Virginia
Feb. 24, 1863

Dear Ann:

After my love to you and the children I received your letter with the post stamps and would have wrote to you sooner but I was looking for another letter from you every day. I am hardly able to get about with my back. I went to the hospital last Friday. We have had plenty of snow here for the last week. It is pleasant here today. I want you to let me know if Lighty did look after that money yet or not. I will have fifty-two dollars to draw next payday. That will be next month. Write to me as soon as this comes to hand. My back hurts me so bad I will have to quit writing now. Lawyer and Will is well. You should not have wrote home about Lawyer leaving for home for you know how your mother frets. He wrote home to her that he hadn't left but he did. He told them he was just to see the 84th regiment that is the one Bill Logan's company is in. You must not show this letter to them or anybody. Please give my respects to all inquiring friends. I would write more but I can't. Nothing more at present but remain your sincere loving husband till death,

John W. Brendel

Let me know how things are about town. Tell Jenny and Bobby I send them a kiss and you give it to them. Tell them to be good children till I come home good by.

Captain Bill Logan enlisted with the 84th Pennsylvania Company C on September 9, 1862. Logan was discharged on August 28, 1863.

The 84th Pennsylvania Regiment that Brendel referred to was organized in the fall of 1861. After the Battle of Bull Run the regiment only had seventy men. The regiment re-joined the army at Berlin (Brunswick) Maryland in October. After the Battle of Fredericksburg, the regiment went into winter quarters near Falmouth. When Maj. General Hooker took command, the regiment was assigned to the Third Corps, Third Division, Third Brigade.[9]

Written to:
Mrs. Anna Brendel, Care of Jacob Brendel
Bellvernow (ed. Belle Vernon), Fayette County, Pa.
(ed. Belle Vernon is located southwest of West Newton)

Camp near Bells Landing Virginia
March Sunday 1st 1863

Dear Anny:

After my love to you and the children I hope these few lines may find you all enjoying good health though I am not very well myself but I feel thankful to God that I am as well as I am. I have the rheumatism (ed. arthritis) and my back is very bad. I can hardly walk with it. It has never been right since the South Mountain fight. I fell over some rock that night and sprained it and I don't know if it will ever get well or not. It is worse now than it has been yet. I have not had any letters from you since I received that one with the three stamps in and I have been looking every day and all in vain. I have been in the hospital since last Friday a week ago. There will be a prayer meeting here tonight at early candle lighting. We was mustered in yesterday for four months pay and I expect we will be paid off about the 15th of this month and I will send you some if God spares my life. But you must try and write to me and let me know if you are living or not. It seems a good while since I heard from you. Direct your letters the same as before. Let me know if you have any money or not and how you are getting along. I want you to let me know if Lighty looked after that bond or not and let me know all about things in particular. You must excuse me from not writing more to you but I don't feel like writing or anything else. Will and Lawyer is both well. Nothing more at present but remain your husband. Truly,

John W. Brendel

Write as soon as this comes to hand.

The terrain at South Mountain is very rugged and steep.

Written to:
Mrs. Ann M. Brendel
West Newton, Westmorland Co. Penna.

Camp near Bells Landing, Virginia
March 8th, 1863

Dear Ann:

After my love to you and family I received your kind letters last night and was very glad to hear from you that you was all well. I thought it was very long to hear from you. It has been three weeks since I had a letter from you. I feel a great deal better today. My back hurts me a great deal and I am very weak. I never have been bedfast yet and I feel very thankful to God for that you spoke of sending me a box and some money. You need not mine that for I can get everything that I want nearly and everything would be spoiled until it would get here. I will send you some money as soon as I get paid off. If I had been paid off I would been home but I want my money first. I will try and get home to see you all as soon as we get paid and I think that will be before long. William and Lawyer are both well. Lawyer had his court martial. His sentence is four months pay to be took off and four months work. He says he won't let them know at home about it but I don't think they will take it off him. I am in our regimental hospital, it is here with the regiment. William Anderson is here on a visit. Liz Brendel is keeping house for him. He says that she is going to get married. Give my love to Jenny, Sammy and Robby and tell them to be good children and

I will send them all some money to buy candy. I think the paymaster will be here about the 15th of this month and I will try for a furlough then. Give my respects to Mont Hays and tell him to write to me and I will answer him right off. Give my respects to all inquiring friends. Nothing more at present but remain your sincere husband,

John W. Brendel

Kiss the children all for me and take one yourself and don't fret about me for I will get along if God spares my life and I hope he will for I put my trust in him and he is my only trust, good by Anny.

Due to the lack of granting leaves of absence, soldiers sometimes took it upon themselves to leave without permission. This, of course, was considered desertion. The punishment for desertion ranged from a fatherly talk to imprisonment and sometimes, even execution.[10]

Written to:
No envelope

Camp near Bells Landing, Virginia
March 18, 1863

Dear Wife:

I received your letter the 15th and was very glad to hear that you was all well. I feel a little better than I was. I have never been bedfast yet, I am able to be about. You wanted to send me some money. You need not mind it. We have a sutler here and I can get anything I want that there is here. It is healthy here. There is two or three cases of small pox in the regiment. They sent them to the division hospital. The paymaster has not been round yet but I look for him shortly. You must get along as well as you can and as quick as I get my pay I will send you some money. Lawyer and will is in good health. If you write to broth-

er Jacob and Lucy tell brother Jacob that I wrote him a letter and received no answer from him yet. Give him the direction for I did not give it right for him for my head was out of order and I hardly knew what I was writing. When I get my money I will try to get a furlough and come home and see you all. There was some heavy cannonading up the Rappahannock yesterday. They said the Rebs was trying to come over. I don't think we will stay much longer here. We have been under marching orders this good while but there is no telling how long we will stay here. I could write to you and tell you about everything but I think I will soon get home and I can tell you all about things in general. Tell Jenny and Sammy that I would like to hear a word from them and one little word from Robby. Kiss them all for me and tell them to be good children till I see them again. Nothing more but my sincere love to you your affectionate husband,

John W. Brendel

Write soon for I have only got two letters from you in about five weeks and I think it long to here from you. Give my well wishes to Mont.

Written to:
Mrs. Ann M. Brendel
West Newton, Westmoreland, Co. Pa.

Camp near Bells Landing, Virginia
March the 22nd, 1863

My Dear Anny:

After my love to you and dear family I would inform you that I received your kind letter dated the 17th and was very glad to hear from you but was sorry to hear that you was not well. I feel a great deal better than I was. I think we will leave here before long. It seems very strange to me that Lighty can't get the money. John Sheppler (ed. Shepler) of our camp got his fifty dollars without any trouble. You go and get them papers and put *them away carefully. I know a lawyer in Pittsburg and I will write to him and then I will let you know what to do with them. You must get along the best you can. I did not get my money yet but I think I will get it before long. Tell Plummer he need not be uneasy about his rent. Tell him that he shall have his money as soon as I get paid off and that will be before long. I saw a Greensburg paper and the list of them that had drawed relief money for 62 and I saw on the list Martha Brindle sixteen dollars but I don't think that was for your name. You can let me know in your next letter how much you drawed if you please. Give my love to the children and take a good portion for yourself and tell them to be good children till their pap comes home and to obey their mother. Write as soon as this comes to hand. You must excuse my strong letters. Nothing more at present, but remain your humble husband,*

John W. Brendel

We can see the Rebs camps from our picket line. They are forty thick. They are on the other side of the Rappahannock River and we are between the Rappahannock and the Potomac Rivers. The weather has been wet and snowy all this month. If it had not been for the rain we would not been here now. But it was so muddy we could not march.

On the back of the letter is written:

Mary Hewitt, East Fairfield, Columbiana Co. Ohio

John Shepler enlisted August 29, 1862, promoted to 1st Sergeant on February 1, 1865 and discharged on May 31, 1865.

Written to:
Mrs. Ann M. Brendel
Westnewton, Westmorland County Penna.

> Camp near Belles Landing
> April 9, 1863

Dear Wife,

After my love to you that I received your kind letter and was very sorry to hear that you was not well but I feel very thankful to God that you are no worse then you are and that I am a great deal better then I was. I received your letter the day before yesterday. I was on guard and came off yesterday. The President was here and our division was out on review but I did not go out. I have seen the old koon [sic] often enough. I thought they had better come to pay the soldiers off we have almost six months pay coming to us now. But we are only mustered in for four months pay if they wait till the first of next month we will get six months pay but they're looking for the paymaster everyday if they had paid off sooner I would have been at home before this time. I think I will get home if they pay off pretty soon I will send you some money as soon as they pay off. I don't think that I can stand soldiering if my back don't get better. My throat and mouth has been sore for two or three weeks and I aint going to do much marching if I don't get better and I don't think that my back will ever get well for it has hurt me ever since the South Mountain fight and that was on the 14th of September a day that I will never forget. That was the first time that I saw the elephant but have saw him twice since (ed. Antietam, Fredericksburg) and hope I maybe so lucky as to never see him again. I would have wrote to you this morning but I was washing today. I had a pretty good wash today I had 12 pieces, cooked breakfast for four of us, dinner and supper and baked corn cakes for breakfast and supper and so I had not time to write to you till tonight and I thought I have got a letter from you this evening when the mail came in but felt very much disappointed when the mail came and no letter. I hope I'll get one soon. If Lighty thinks he can not get that money in Pittsburg you can go and get them papers and put them away safe and I know a *lawyer in Pittsburg and I will write to him and get him to attend to it. Let me know in your next letter if you got the papers back then I will write to the lawyer and get him to collect it. It is after nine o clock now and I feel a little tired after a hard day's washing. So you must excuse my scribbling tonight give my love to the children and take a great big heap of it for yourself. Give my love to all enquiring friends and tell Mont that I never received that letter from him yet. Good night nothing more at present but remain your true and loving husband. Will and Lawyer is both well and send their love to you. They got a box of nice things from home some weeks ago. Lawyer gave me two onions and Will give me my supper one night when he opened a can of peaches.*

John W. Brendel

In early April, President Lincoln, his wife Mary and Attorney General Bates reviewed more than sixty-thousand of General Hooker's soldiers. The president rode on a large bay horse most of the time. One soldier noted that his appearance was "not very graceful, and hardly calculated to inspire much admiration." Lincoln seemed impressed by the army's readiness. "Uniforms were clean, arms bright as new, equipment in splendid condition."[11]

Paymasters were military accountants. A paymaster's safe was made of iron to keep money and documents secure from theft and fire.[12]

Written to:
Mrs. Anne M. Brendel
Westnewton, Westmoreland Co. Penna.

Camp near Bells Landing
April 13th 1863

Dear Wife:

After my love to you and family I feel very thankful to God that I am pretty well with the exception of my back and I don't know whether it will ever get better here. But I hope these few lines may find you and family enjoying good health. I have been looking every day for a letter from you for better than a week but looked all in vain. I think you have fell in love with someone else and have forgotten me. I don't expect we will be here long. The cavalry is all moving now. I see in the papers that the paymaster has been started out to pay the Army of the Potomac off. I hope they will reach us before long. If they don't reach here by the first of the month we will have six months pay to draw. I think it is time that they come. The old regiments are to be consolidated and the over surplus of commissioned and non-commissioned officers are to be mustered out of service and I think I stand a good chance to be mustered out. We have four corporals and we only want two if consolidated. So I think my chance is good. If I ain't mustered out I will get a furlough and come home. There is two out of every hundred can go at one time out of the regiment. That makes four out of our regiment at once. So it will soon be my turn. If I would have got my money sooner I would have been home before this. If we start on a march you must not be uneasy when you don't get my letters from me. For we don't get mail sometimes for a week or more and have no chance to write. You will have to do the best you can for money till I send you some and that will be before long. I think I will be paid in two or three days. The right name of this camp is camp near Fletchers Chapel. The church is about four hundred yards from here. We have made a brigade hospital out of it. The health of the army is good. We have had fourteen cases of smallpox in our brigade and three of them died. There is no more cases now. There is nothing of any importance to write to you so I shall quit and not write till I get some word from you. I think you are a little neglectful about writing. Nothing more at present, give my love to the children and tell them to be good children for pap's sake till he comes home. My love to you your faithful husband,

John W. Brendel

This is a soldier's letter. We can't get any stamps here for love or money. I did not get them stamps you sent me. Try and write as soon as these few lines come to hand.

Smallpox is a contagious virus with no specific treatment. The name comes from the Latin word "spotted" because the patient has raised bumps on the face and body. Generally, the virus spreads by face-to-face contact. Including the incubation period the virus can last over one month.[13]

Written to:
No envelope

Camp near Bells Landing, Virginia
April the 15th, 1863

Dear Anny,

I am well this evening, only my back and I hope these few lines may find you and family enjoying good health. I got a letter yesterday dated Feb. 17th but have not got any letter from you for about three weeks and I think it is along time to hear from you. The last letter I got from you, you had all been sick and I would like very much to hear from you but it appears that I cannot. I sometimes think you have forgotten me. But I hope you will soon write. We are under marching orders now with five days rations in our knapsacks and haversacks. Where we are going I cannot tell. I suppose we would have been off this morning but it commenced raining last night about 12 o'clock and has rained ever since. But I think we will be off tomorrow. If you don't get any letters from me when we are on a march. You must not be uneasy for we can't get any chance to send any letters off. I think we will be paid off before we leave here. The paymaster is here and has paid off some regiments in this division yesterday and if he pays off before we leave I will send you my money home. The boys are well. I have written so much from here that there is nothing interesting to write about. I was on camp guard yesterday and came off this morning at 9 o'clock. I made Jenny a ring out of a piece of laurel root off the Battlefield of Antietam. I placed my guard around the camp and then sat down and made the ring between times. When you look at the ring you can think of me and the bloody battlefield of Antietam where thousands were slain. The health of the army is good. The men are in good spirits but don't care about having another fight if it could be helped. The first of this month was snowing or raining nearly every day. It has been pleasant the last few days. It is not cold here to night. I am sitting writing in my shirt sleeves and am comfortable. So it is going on 10 o'clock I will bid you goodnight for I did not sleep much last night for I was at my post like a soldier. You must excuse my bad writing and mistakes. Give my love to the children and keep a good portion for yourself and I hope by the grace of God to see you all before long and then I can tell you all about war. Nothing more at present but remain your loving husband,

John W. Brendel

Give Jenny the ring and tell her to keep it sheen. Put it on her finger and wear it. Tell Sammy I will make him one as soon as I can.

There were two main types of haversacks - canvas and oil cloth. While supposedly waterproof, both were no more effective than plain cloth for repelling water. Haversacks carried all kinds of food. Examples of usual content included: salt pork, salted beef, greasy bacon various kinds of vegetables and hardtack. Imagine the smell of a haversack after a military campaign. Haversacks were slung over the right shoulder and rested on the left hip.

The knapsack was made of painted canvas. In addition to the food that Brendel mentions, most knapsacks contained a rubber blanket, wool blanket and a shelter tent half. The rubber blanket laid on the ground prevented moisture from penetrating the wool blanket. The other half of the shelter tent was carried by another soldier. At night, the two buttoned the halves together and shared the tent.[14]

Written to:
Mrs. Ann M. Brendel
Bellvirman (ed. Belle Vernon), Fayette County, Penna.

Camp near Fletchers Chapel
April the 29, 1863

After my love to you and family, I am well and hope you are enjoying the same blessing. We are all faced up for a march this morning. I sent you twenty-five dollars by the chaplain to the express office yesterday. I will write as soon as I can. I have not time this morning, your husband,

John W. Brendel

Here is Sam's candy money twenty-five cents.

(Written on the back of the letter):

Mr. Brendel and me is coming home some day before war is over. We have lots of fun here. J.Gregg (ed. John Gregg mustered in August 28, 1862, wounded December 13, 1862, died of wounds received in action, April 1, 1865)

After four months of relative inactivity due to inclement weather conditions, the Union's new commanding general, Joseph Hooker, took the Union army on the offensive. The objective of the campaign was to attack the Confederates left flank south of the Rappahannock River.

On April 27, Hooker sent three Corps northwest along the Rappahannock towards Kelly's Ford. As a diversion tactic on April 29, three Corps (including the 11th Pennsylvania) was dispatched south below Fredericksburg to give the impression that the real attack would be on the Confederate right.[15]

Written to:
No envelope

Near Fredericksburg
April 30, 1863

Dear Anny:

I thought I would drop you a few lines to let you know we have moved. We are crossing the Rappahannock. Commenced crossing yesterday, three of our division was killed and about thirty wounded and took about one hundred prisoners May 1. We had a shelling yesterday. I have not time to write. I send you twenty-five dollars by the chaplain last Monday. I will write as soon as I can. Try and write a little more than you do. I am in good heart this time. I think we will wail them this time,

John W. Brendel

On May 2, the First Corps was re-assigned to the battle that was taking place near Chancellorsville. The First Corps proceeded northwest past Falmouth twelve miles to the U. S. Ford crossing of the Rappahannock River. The First Corps was placed on the right flank of the Union army. On the May 2, the breastworks were strengthened.[16]

Written to:
No envelope

May 4th, 1863

Dear Wife:

Thank God I am well this morning. I received a letter from you this morning and was glad to hear from you. We are sixteen miles above Fredericksburg. Came here Saturday evening had two good shellings [sic] below Fredericksburg. They were fighting here when we came. We have been laying in line of battle ever since we came. We hold the right of the line. I think we will give them a good wailing this time. There has not been a man hurt yet. I feel in good spirits and think by the help of God we will do it up right this time. I have got no letter from you since we left the old camp but this one this morning. I don't want you to fret about me. I am in good spirits and hope God will take care of me and my little family. The boys are well. Here is a little book I made the last day was on post at the old camp. I will quit writing for I have no time to write. I sent twenty-five dollars to the express office by the chaplain but I don't think he has got there yet on account of this battle. He has to have a pass. Dear Anny here is twenty-five cents for Bobby and tell Jenny I will send her more to get a dress. I think I will be at home when this battle is over. It has been going on for about six days now. My love to you all, write immediately your husband,

John W. Brendel

In the line of battle now writing good-by.

During the late afternoon of May 2, the right flank of the Union army received a surprise attack by Thomas Jonathan (Stonewall) Jackson's Corps. The Eleventh Corps was repulsed during the attack. At the end of the day while performing reconnaissance the infamous Stonewall Jackson was mortally wounded. This would prove to be a severe blow for the leadership of the Confederacy.[17]

On May 3, the First Corps breastworks were strengthened. At 4 p.m. the 11th, Pennsylvania was on the skirmish line where they remained until May 6. On May 6, the Union army began to retreat back cross the Rappahannock River. The 11th Pennsylvania was the last to cross at the U.S. Ford. The 11th Pennsylvania returned to camp near Falmouth.[18]

The Union outnumbered the Confederates 130,000 to 60,000 during the Chancellorsville Campaign but still lost the battle.[19]

Written to:
No envelope

Virginia
May the 15, 1863

Dear Wife:

I received your letter dated May 5 and was very glad to hear from you that you was all well. I don't feel very well this morning but I hope to God that these few lines may find you enjoying good health. I hope you will get them twenty-five dollars I sent you before these few lines reaches you. The preacher has left this morning for the express office. I have sent Jenny sixty and Sammy twenty-five and Robby twenty-five cents and you a little bone bible I made for a memorial and have not heard whether you got them or not. We have not drawed the balance of our money yet. But when I draw it I will try and send you twenty-five dollars more. We packed up this morning for another march but the order was countermanded. Nothing more at present but remain your loving husband,

John W. Brendel

I will not write until I get an answer from you.

After the Battle of Chancellorsville the 11th Pennsylvania was re-assigned to the First Corps, Second Division, Second Brigade.[20]

Written to:
Mrs. Ann M. Brendel
Westnewton, Westmoreland, Co. Penna.

> Camp 11th Regt. P.V.
> Near the old camp, Virginia
> May 31, 1863

Dear Wife:

I received three letters since I wrote you one and I will give you my reason for not writing sooner because I had written you two or three and had not got an answer from you and Friday when I received the last one I was out on picket and Saturday our Corps was on review and I had not time to write any sooner. We are not here like at home. We must do as we can not as we please. I am not very well at present but am very thankful to God that you are all well. I was glad to hear that you had got that money for it had been long enough. Two regiments in our brigade got paid off while we were out on pickets and I expect we will be paid off in a few days. I don't know if there will be any more furloughs give or not. There has been none given since this last battle. Our regiment stood out in the front line forty-eight hours and not a shot fired at us. The 136th run when there was a few shots fired at them and we checked them and the general's aide told us if they run again to make them do our fighting. When we came back to the breastworks we had thrown up the night before we went out, the whole army had gone and nearly all over the river again. It looked a little squirrelly. They did not throw a shell at us when we crossed but we had two good shellings [sic] below Fredericksburg but not one hurt in our regiment. There was four or five killed in our brigade and eight or nine wounded. So I think we got off well. The weather is dry here. We have had no rain of any amount for five or six weeks. Fruit has the appearance of being plenty if nothing happens to it. I wish the war was over and then I would like to come home but I think it will be settled before many months more. Our Potomac army have lost between thirty and forty thousand troops since the last battle. Some two-year regiments and some nine-month regiments have gone home and there was a great many wounded in *the last battle. This is so close to the camp to have anything interesting to write about so I think I will quit for the present and the quicker you write the sooner you will get a answer. Give my respects to all inquiring friend and tell me all the particulars about town. You wanted, you always ask me for a likeness. I told you three or four times I would send it to you as soon as I could get it taken. Give my love to the children and take a good portion for yourself and write as soon as this comes to hand, Nothing more at present but remain your loving husband,*

John W. Brendel

During this period in time, the Union Army was mainly comprised of three-year soldiers. However, there were also two-year soldiers and nine-month soldiers whose terms were expiring.

Between April and June, the Union lost twenty-three thousand soldiers due to expired enlistment terms. Soldiers were reluctant to re-enlist immediately, due in part to the Enrollment Act of March 3, 1863 (Draft). Under the act, a draftee could escape service if he paid a three-hundred dollar fee or provided a substitute. If a veteran soldier waited to re-enlist, he could make three-hundred dollars as a substitute. At the time, three-hundred dollars was the average yearly salary for a laborer.[21]

On June 3, the Confederate Infantry moved from Fredericksburg to the area of Culpeper beginning the Gettysburg Campaign. On June 10, General Richard Ewell's Corps leading the advance of the army proceeded north and west across the Blue Ridge Mountains and into the Shenandoah Valley. Most of the Confederates crossed the Potomac River at Shepherdstown and Williamsport advancing towards the north in Union territory.

By June 12, the Union Army was proceeding north along the Bull Run Mountains attempting to position themselves between the Confederates and Washington. Extreme heat and hard marching would make this one of the army's most difficult marches.⁽²²⁾ With little time to eat or sleep, and marching as far as thirty-five miles a day under the scorching sun over dust filled roads, there is no wonder why Brendel did not write home during this period.

After passing through Warrenton Junction, Centreville, Herndon and Guilford Station, the 11th Pennsylvania crossed the Potomac River at Edwards Ferry on June 25. Continuing through Barnesville, Middletown and Emmittsburg, the regiment camped at the Wolford farm located on the Maryland/Pennsylvania state line (Mason& Dixon line).⁽²³⁾

On June 27, in the middle the Confederate invasion to the north, General Hooker resigned as commander. Hooker resigned over a dispute with General-in-Chief of the Land Forces of the United States, Henry W. Halleck. Hooker suggested that Union forces at Harpers Ferry reinforce the Army of the Potomac. Hooker told Halleck he could not cover both Harpers Ferry and Washington.

General George Gordon Meade replaced Hooker as the commander of the Army of the Potomac.⁽²⁴⁾ General Meade was a native of Pennsylvania. When the 11th Pennsylvania received word of Meade's appointment, and upon entering Pennsylvania, three cheers were given.⁽²⁵⁾

At 9 a.m. on the morning of July 1, the 11th Pennsylvania proceeded north towards Gettysburg. They were heading to what would become the largest battle in the history of North America.

The 11th Pennsylvania had just come off picket duty so they were the last regiment in the column of the First Corps. The regiment could hear the enemy artillery as they approached the battlefield.

During the Battle of Gettysburg, the 11th Pennsylvania was assigned to the First Corps (Maj. Generals Reynolds, KIA, Doubleday and eventually Newton), Second Division (Robinson), Second Brigade (Baxter). Later in the day on July 1, the 11th Pennsylvania was reassigned to the First Brigade (Coulter).

Arriving on the battlefield at Seminary Ridge, the 11th Pennsylvania formed north of the Seminary between the Chambersburg Pike and Mummasburg Road at approximately 1 p.m. The enemy to the front comprised parts of Rodes Division consisting of Iverson's North Carolina troops and O'Neal's Alabama troops.

Iverson's Brigade advanced towards the well-hidden Union troops. When Iverson's troops were within one-hundred yards, Baxter's Brigade rose up and delivered a withering fire. Baxter's Brigade then advanced forward, capturing one-thousand men and three battle flags of Iverson's Brigade.[26]

Afterwards, Baxter's Brigade went in support of Battery B, 4th United States Artillery.[27] Confederate reinforcements forced the Union army through the streets of Gettysburg. The 11th Pennsylvania retreated in fairly good order, according to Regimental Chaplain William Locke: "Shoulder to shoulder they marched, rank after rank; halting to fire upon the advancing foe, and then closing up again with daring coolness." Unfortunately, they also ran into the chaos of the town.[28] The streets were filled with retreating soldiers. The 11th Pennsylvania spent the night of July 1 constructing breastworks on the south side of Gettysburg on Cemetery Hill.

On the morning of July 2, the First Brigade was relieved by the Second Corps, Third Division and went to the rear in support of batteries on Cemetery Hill. At sunset, they were assigned to support the Third Corps but returned later to once again support the Eleventh Corps.

On July 3, the Brigade moved to the rear of the cemetery in support of the Twelfth Corps. At 2 p.m. they were assigned to assist a battery on the right and rear of the Second Corps, Third Division during the Confederate assault which would become known as Picket's Charge (Confederate Maj. General George E. Picket 1825-1875). The First Brigade remained in this position until the close of the battle. The brigade went into battle with less than 1,200 men.[29]

Geddisburg Penna July 5th 1863
Dear wife
After my love to you and family I would inform you that I am as well as can be expected we have had 3 days hard fighting the 1st 2 and 3 of July I just droped you a fiew lines to let you know that I am still living I have no more time to wright to you the mail is ready to start out and we must follow the Rebs
your Faithfull Husband
John W Brendel
we have only had 2 mails since we started from the old Camp and only got 2 letters from you one to day wright soon and often yo

Original letter written by John W. Brendel while still on the battlefield at Gettysburg.

Written to:
Mrs. Ann M. Brendel
Westnewton, Westmoreland Co. Penna.

Geddisburg [sic], Penna.
July 5, 1863

Dear Wife:

After my love to you and family I would inform you that I am as well as can be expected. We have had three days hard fighting the first, second, and third of July. I just dropped you a few lines to let you know that I am still living. I have no more time to you the mail is ready to start out and we must follow the Rebels. Your faithful husband,

John W. Brendel

We have only had two mails since we started from the old camp and only got two letters from you one today write soon and often. I will write as soon as I can.

After receiving a crushing defeat at Gettysburg on July 3, Robert E. Lee's Confederate army began a long retreat towards Virginia the following day. Torrential rains hindered the seventeen-mile long wagon train as it snaked southward west of the Catoctin Mountains.

While Lee's intention was to cross the Potomac River at Williamsport, Maryland, heavy rains had brought the river to flood stage. The circumstances forced the Confederates to put up nine miles of defenses from just west of Hagerstown, Maryland to the Potomac River south of Williamsport.[30]

During the same time period, the Union infantry proceeded south along the eastern side of the Catoctin Mountains to a converging point at Frederick, Maryland. General Meade's intention was to keep the Union army between his forces and Washington/Baltimore.

From Frederick, the Union army headed west through the area of the old South Mountain Battlefield. It was in this area on September 14, 1862 where Brendel saw the elephant for the first time.

The 11th Pennsylvania bivouacked on the north side of South Mountain on July 8-9. By July 12, the regiment had crossed the Antietam Creek at Funkstown, Maryland, formed in line of battle and entrenched during the evening.[31]

Written to:
Mrs. Ann Brendel
West Newton, Westmorland County, Penna.
*Soldiers Letter

Near Antietam
July 11, 1863

Dear Wife,

I sit down to drop you a few lines to let you know that I am still living and feel very thankful to God for his kindness to me for bringing me safe this far through this last battle. We had three days hard fighting at Gettysburg and gave the Rebs a good whipping and we have them cornered here again and laying in the line of battle to give it to them again for I think we can by the help of God. You must excuse me for not writing more to you for I don't feel much like writing or anything else. You must write as soon as this comes to hand. Give my love to the children. The boys are well. Colonel Coulter was wounded in the arm on the second day's fight. Nothing more at present but remain your loving husband.

John W. Brendel

After consulting with his senior commanders on July 12, Meade sent out a reconnaissance in force on the morning of July 14, only to discover that the Confederates had crossed the river at Williamsport and Falling Waters overnight.

The Confederate crossing of the Potomac River ended the Gettysburg Campaign. The 11th Pennsylvania had passed through Keedysville, Maryland near the site of the Battle of Antietam ten months earlier. On July 18, the 11th Pennsylvania crossed the Potomac River once again at Berlin (Brunswick) returning to Virginia. The regiment returned to the Second Brigade.[32]

Written to:
Mrs. Ann Brendel
West Newton, Westmorland County, Penna.
*Soldiers Letter- Due 6 Cents

Middleburg Virginia
July 22, 1863

Dear Anny,

I sit down to drop you a few lines to let you know that I am still living and not very well but I hope to God these few lines may find you all well. I think you have forgotten me I have only got one letter from you this month that was dated July 1st and I think it very long to hear from you. I would like to write to you all about the last battle but I have not time and seldom we can get a letter in the mail. We don't get the mail often this is a real sesesh (ed. seethe or excited) town. They are all sesesh [sic] here. You must try and write to me a little oftener then you do for you know that is all the pleasure I have when I hear from you. You must excuse me for not writing more to you but I don't feel like writing. My love to you and the children kiss them for me, your affectionate husband,

John W. Brendel

The following letter is written on the same paper as the previous letter:

Warrenton, Virg.
July 24

Dear Wife:

We started from Middleburg day before yesterday and marched all night and got here yesterday and in camp but I don't know how long we will stay here. I wrote you five letters since the Gettysburg fight but don't know whether you got any of them or not. But I tell you we had three days hard fighting there. Six of our company was taken prisoner, three wounded. The captain is with us the two lieutenants was wounded. We have one commissioned officer and two non-commissioned officers, the orderly and myself (ed. corporal). So there is three of us to manage the company but there is only eleven men in the company now. Dear Anny I want you to write soon and often, yours in heart. The mail is going out, now I must quit.

J.W. Brendel

Written to:
No envelope

Camp Union across the
Rappahannock River at the Station
August 4, 1863

Dear Wife:

My love to you and family. I am well at present and feel very thankful. I received a letter from you this morning and was very glad to here from you. We crossed the river last Saturday and drove the Rebs back to Culpeper and we have been looking for them to attack us every day. They advanced on us about a mile on Sunday. We have the hills all fortified and will give them a good time if they come to us here. We are in line of battle now. I *have not time to write much to you. You may send me one dollar in your next letter. I have no tobacco or money either. We did not get our money yet and don't think there will be much coming to us for we drawed two suits of clothes and was ordered to send them back to Washington but I think the government will pay us for them. My clothing is sixty some dollars so that will leave but little to get when we are paid. You will have to live saving if you can. You need not send the dollar unless you have it to spare. So my love to my dear wife, your affectionate husband,*

John W. Brendel

Write soon and often.

It was by design that the army was encamped near the railroad. Supplies were delivered to the army from Washington on the Orange & Alexandria Railroad.(33)

Written to:
No envelope

Camp across the river opposite the Rappahannock Station, Virginia August the 14, 1863

Dear Wife:

After my love to you and family I would inform you that I received your letter and was very thankful to God for your health and my own. I am well with the exceptions of my back and I don't think it will ever be any better. It pains me so at night that I cannot half sleep at night. I received one dollar and had the notion to send it back to you, the next time I send to you for a dollar if you have it to spare. You won't growl about it, that is providing I keep my health. I would not wrote to you for that if I had been well. I had not been well one hour since we left South Mountain and that will be one year against the 14th of next month and it cost me a good deal of money when I was sick. I could not eat salt pork or hardtack. It keeps me busy enough to eat when I am well. I think if some of you was here to live on the kind of grub we have to live on you would not think we spent our money gambling. My clothing bill is about seventy dollars in place of sixty. We did not settle the last two months clothing. We got forty-two dollars a year for our clothes. I told you in my other letter the clothing we drawed in Harrisburg. We were all ordered to send back and did and came on to Antietam and drawed another suite and at Bell Plain Landing was ordered to send that suite back and had the two to pay for besides what I wore out. The officers says the government will pay us for them. If it does it is well and if not they can keep it. I can live without it. I suppose it was hardly worthwhile to tell you about it for you appeared to know more about what it took to keep me than I did myself. I think someone has informed you wrong. If so they had better attend to there own business and I will attend to mine. Were encamped opposite the Rappahannock Station. The day after I wrote to you we had a little skirmish with the Rebs and made them get up and dust. Enclosed you will find a song you can sing when you feel merry. My sincere love to you and my dear children. My sheet is a full one. I would tell you a heap more. The boys are well. Write soon, your true and loving husband,

John W. Brendel

The word skirmish is an old French word meaning sword fighting. During the Civil War era, it had nothing to do with sword fighting. Skirmish meant reaching out to make contact with the enemy. A company could be sent out in front of a regiment to gauge the enemy and draw fire which may start a general engagement. Being situated between the enemy and your own army was dangerous. Soldiers would sometimes fight with no notice, get pinned down under enemy fire or run for their lives.[34]

Written to:
Mrs. Ann M. Brendel
Westnewton, Westmoreland County, Penna.

Rappahannock Station, Virginia
Camp 11th Reg., Graveyard Hill
August 15, 1863

Dear Wife:

I take my pencil in hand to inform you that I am well and hope you are enjoying the same blessing. My dear wife we are under marching orders with three days cooked rations. I wrote you a letter yesterday and it may be possible you will be offended at it but you must for I thought you disputed my word. I don't think I ever told you a lie in earnest in my life. I suppose I can tell what things cost when I have them to pay as well as anybody can tell me. So excuse me and let all these little foolish things drop. I thought I would drop you a few lines to let you know that we were a going to move again. I want you to write a little oftener than you did when we was on the last march. I wrote to you every chance I had and that was not very often. I was over the river to see the reserves and Gust Fox told me that man Neff and John was taken prisoner at Gettysburg and you said Andy Neff was at home on a furlough. I thought you wrote to me long ago he was discharged. There is no particular news to write to you for you know as much about the Army of the Potomac as we do. They have brought about eight-hundred conscripts to this Corps and about one-half of them is pick pockets. They bring them here under guard. There was three of them shot by the guard for trying to run off. There was three-hundred came here last night. I don't know what kind of soldiers they will make but I think in a general way they will make poor soldiers. It did not take a guard to bring us old veterans out. So good by, I will send Robby a little book. If you did not get that money from Lighty, I want you to get it and when you want anything you haven't got to go and ask for it. Give me all the particulars about town. Give my respects to all inquiring friends. Tell Monty Hays that I am very sorry to here that he has took to drinking again. My sincere love to you my dear wife and my week prayers to you and me *until we meet again and my prayers is to God it will be before long. Kiss the children for me. May God spare us to meet. Your affectionate husband,*

John W. Brendel

I must stop.

On July 4, General Lee proposed an exchange of prisoners with General Meade. Lee claimed the proposal would promote their comfort and convenience. While uncertain, Lee's real reason may have been that he did not want the burden of guarding and feeding the Union soldiers. Meade refused the offer, stating that such proceedings were not under his jurisdiction. Lee had already paroled fifteen-hundred soldiers of the First Corps and sent them by escort to Carlisle.[35]

Lee took nearly four-thousand Union soldiers with him back to Virginia. Some of these soldiers were imprisoned at Belle Isle Prison. Belle Isle was located on the James River near Richmond; it became a prison after the first Battle of Bull Run in 1861.

Belle Isle was intended to hold three-thousand soldiers but it actually held more than twice that amount. The living conditions of prison were horrendous. Soldiers slept in clusters of tents. The quantity and quality of food was very poor and sanitary conditions were inhuman. One soldier commented that there was "a good deal of fighting going on among the men; just like many hungry wolves penned together." From fifteen to twenty-five prisoners died in the prison each day.[36] These poor conditions were typical of Civil War prisons of both armies.

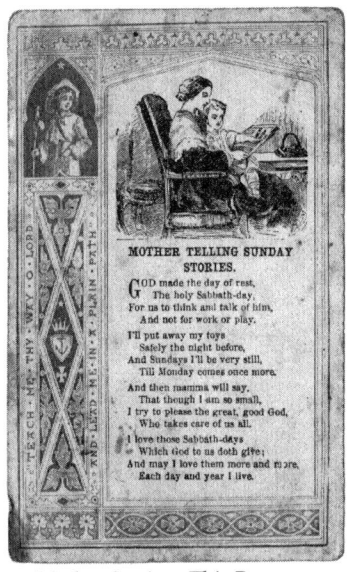

Mother Stories - This Poem was included in the August 21, 1863 letter

Written to:
Mrs. Ann M. Brendel
Westnewton, Westmoreland County, Penna.
*Soldiers Letter - Due 3 Cents

Rappahannock Station
August 21, 1863

Dear Anny:

I received your letter of the 18th and was sorry to here that you took it so hard about the letter I wrote to you on the 14th. I was not angry about the letter you wrote me at all but I would sooner have nothing than to have any parlay about it. So if I hurt your feelings you must forgive me for I humbly beg pardon for so doing so. We will drop it for my love is as strong for you as ever. It was and I am sure that you know that I love you. We crossed the river back to Rappahannock Station again. We are about a mile back from where we were. I don't think the Rebs will show us any fight here. They are drawing their forces back towards Fredericksburg again. William Fox is dead but he did not die in Richmond. He died in Annapolis. I don't think John or Manual Neff was killed at Gettysburg. They were both taken prisoner and took to Richmond. I see Gust Fox nearly every day he is well. The boys are well. I will give you a little advise. You had better get your money again and keep it and when you want it you won't have no trouble running after it. I would not lend money to my father. When I did not know what minute I would want it, so I don't want you to think hard of me giving you a little piece of advice when you have none. Your friends are scarce. I want you in your next to let me know how much money you have and if Irvin Frithman ever paid you that money or not. If there is anything I write amiss I want you to look over it and not your feelings be hurt for it is not my intention to hurt your feelings at all. As for women in the army they are scarce. I have only met four that belong to the army and I don't think they are much or they would not follow the army and for them short letters that I wrote to you, when I wrote them I hardly had time to write that much. I just wrote that to you to let you know that I was still living and very thankful to God that I was. So *you must take all things into consideration and think. I have not the opportunity of writing that you have at home. When the bugle sounds we must all jump, no difference to what is going on. It is going on 10 o'clock my paper is all no more. Give my love to the children and keep a good portion for yourself. Your affectionate husband,*

John W. Brendel

Answer soon.

Written to:
Mrs. Ann M. Brendel
Westnewton, Westmoreland Co. Penna.

My Dear wife this is Saturday Aug. the 22 and I am not very well. I have the diarrhea again. I have been taking medicine the last three days and feel better this morning and feel very thankful to the great creator that I feel as well as I do and I hope to God these few scribbled lines may find you enjoying good health. The weather has been very hot since the 1st of July. The hottest I think I ever felt. We had a little shower of rain last night and cooled the air a little bit but the sun came out very hot again this morning. It is going to be hot today. There is five regiments in our brigade. They have all got conscripts but us and the 97th New York. The 9th New York got two hundred men yesterday morning. Very nice quiet men and I think they will make good soldiers. Our officers is gone to Harrisburg nearly a month ago for our conscripts but have not returned yet with them. So I don't know whether we will get any or not. I wish we would not get any for they are a good lock of bother to an old regiment. The 12th Mass. got theirs and they were all nearly a band of thieves and robbers. Such soldiers I do not want. Tell brother Jacob I wrote him a letter four months ago and he answered it so well I will soon write him another. Tell him that I like to write letters to one that answers them so well as he does. I think I must stop for this time for fear I hurt your feelings again and that I would not do for ten-thousand worlds if I can help it. So if there is anything in this letter to hurt your feelings my dear beloved wife, I beg ten-thousand pardons for it and if there is anything wrong I want you to tell me what it is and you oblige your humble husband. So my dear wife I will quit for this time and want you to write as soon as this comes to hand and not think because my letters are short that I don't love you or that I have fell in love with some other woman. I don't think much of these army straps as to fall in love with them. I am not so easy love stricken as that comto? [sic] Nothing more at present but remain your humble husband until death.

John W. Brendel

Excuse my bad scribbling and mistakes, write soon

Written to:
Mrs. Ann M. Brendel
Westnewton, Westmoreland County, Penna.
*Soldiers Letter

> *Rappahannock Station, Va. Camp 11th Reigt. P.V*
> *Sunday, August 30, 1863*

Dear Wife:

I received your kind letter of the 21st and was very glad to here that you was all well. For there is nothing does me so much good as to hear from you and that you are all well. I feel about as usual. I am taking medicine again for the diarrhea and I feel a little better this morning. I would have wrote to you sooner but I was looking for another letter from you and did not get it yet and thought I would write to you. You wanted to know when our time would be out. The regiment time will be up in April next and company G goes out with the regiment. So that will not be very long. You wanted to know when I would be at home. I expect to be home in about two months if God spares my life and health and I feel God will spare me to get home once more for he has brought me through many hard roads where thousands fell by my side and I am still here and know one knows how thankful I feel to him for his goodness to me. I will stop now for I cannot express my feeling. I will give you some of the army news. There were five deserters shot yesterday in the first division of the Fifth Corps. I did not go to see the poor fellows shot. I thought I had saw as many shot as I wanted to see. They brought four deserters back that belonged to our regiment. They have them under guard. Some of them deserted at Camp Curtin before the regiment came out in the field. We will be mustered in tomorrow for two months pay. The boys are well and I have not seen anything of that box with the tobacco in yet. I bought eight small plugs of tobacco yesterday and paid one dollar for them. When I was at home I could have bought them for twenty-five cents. I have had no laurel root yet but as soon as I can get some I will make you a ring. I will send you a little book that you cannot help but think of me when you look to a throne of grace. Give my love to my dear little children and kiss them for me. Tell them to be good children. My love to you my dear wife. No more at present but remain your affectionate husband,

John W. Brendel

Write soon as this comes to hand.

Written to:
Mrs. Ann M. Brendel
Westnewton, Westmoreland Co. Penna.

Camp 11th Regt. PV. Rappahannock Station
Sept. 6th, 1863

Dear Anny:

After my love to you and family I received your kind and very short letter but was glad to hear from you and was very sorry to hear that you was not well. But I hope to God that you will be restored to your health again. I am not very well myself. I have had my back cupped three days in succession and it don't appear to do me any good yet. But I hope it may for this is a hard place to be when a person is not well. This is Sunday but you would not know the difference between it and a weekday if it was not for inspection. We have inspection every Sunday morning. It is all quiet along the Rappahannock. The Rebs cavalry made a dash down to the river last Friday and fired at our pickets and wounded one slightly and retreated and have not been seen since. I don't think we will have any fight here for I think the Rebs got a plenty the last time they crossed into Pennsylvania. There is nothing of any importance to write to you. So I think I shall stop at this time. I wrote you a long letter and got no answer to it yet. It is very likely you did not get it yet for I directed it to West Newton. You told me in your last letter you did not know whether you would stay in Bellvirnan (ed. Belle Vernon) very long so I can't tell where you want me to direct my letters to. Tell brother Jacob that I am very much obliged to him for that kind answer he wrote to that letter I wrote to him six months ago or maybe more. My love to Jacob and his family. Tell Will and Wiss I send my love to them and I think they might write a word or two to their uncle. But tell them if they know which side of the bread is buttered they had better stay out of the army. My love to you my dear wife. Your affectionate husband,

John W. Brendel

I expect we will be paid off in a week or two. We were mustered in for two months pay the last day of August. Write as soon as this comes to hand and let we know where you are. The captain has put in for a furlough and if he gets it he will be home in a few days and he said that he would stop to see you. But I told him you was in Bellvirnin (ed. Belle Vernon) and he said he would not get to see you. So if you should chance to be at home I want you to invite him to stay and dine with you if you have anything to eat for he has always been very clever to me.

In the last letter, Brendel mentions getting his back cupped 3 times. Cupping was a procedure used to lessen lung pain or pneumonia. The cup was filled with alcohol. The alcohol was ignited and the cup was pressed against the skin. A blister was raised and then was lanced. In reality, the procedure cured nothing.[37]

Written to:
Mrs. Ann M. Brendel
Bellvirnin (Belle Vernon), Fayette Co. Penna.

Camp 11th Regt. PV.
Rappahannock Station
Sept. 15, 1863

Dear Anny:

I received yours of the 5th and was very glad to hear from you. I had not time to answer you sooner. I have been out on picket for three days and we had general inspection and that took another day. Our forces attacked the Rebs on Sunday morning and drove them back beyond the Rappahannock River. The cavalry and two corps of infantry was in front on picket We could see the commencement. We were in sight of their picket line. You must excuse me for not writing more but I don't feel well nor like writing or anything else. I expressed ten dollars to you this morning by Adams Express from Bealeton Station to West Newton. I received the pin cushion and tobacco and the contents and it was very nice. Got it last evening when I came off picket. Excuse my scribbling. You wanted to know if I had written that letter. I did all my own writing myself and I expect you think it poor writing but we have a poor chance here for writing. So you must excuse it. Your affectionate husband,

John W. Brendel

The old Corporal

Here is twenty cents for Robb and Jenny for to take a spree on. To do what they please with, if Bob wants candy.

Written to:
Mrs. Ann M. Brendel
Bellvirnin (Belle Vernon), Fayette Co. Penna.

Camp near Culpeper Court House
September 22, 1863

Dear Wife:

I received your kind letter of the 11th and was glad to hear from you. We crossed the Rappahannock today one week ago and are going towards the Rapidan River. We got marching orders last night and eight days rations and expect to move every hour. You must excuse me for not writing sooner but I had not time. The orderly sergeant is sick and I had to take charge of the camp. We have to drill twice every day and dress parade at sunset. I expressed ten dollars at Bealeton Station before we left there and wrote to you and sent Jenny and Robb some change and have received no answer from you yet. I sent the money to West Newton. Give my love to Ell and Jacob and family and tell them I hope to be at home before long. I will answer Ell's letter as soon as I get time. You must write to me often for when we are on a march I cannot write to you. No mail goes out no more my dear wife but remain your loving husband,

John W. Brendel

Written to:
Mrs. Ann M. Brendel
West Newton, Westmorland County, Penna.
*Soldiers Letter - Due 3 Cents

Camp 11 Regt. Near Rapidan River
October 1, 1863

Dear Wife:

I received your kind and welcome letter and thought you was long about writing. We moved closer to the Rebs they are throw-

ing up breast-works on the other side of the river. Our pickets have been over and traded newspapers with them and tobacco and was very sociable with others and they hoped the day might soon come when we could talk to each other again and so do I. Dear Ann, I feel a little better today then I did. I haven't been well for some time I will come home as soon as I can. I will try to come home when we get into winter quarters and I think that will be before very long. The nights are cool here now. We had several hard frosts here. You must excuse me for not writing more to you but there is nothing here to write about of any importance. Give my love to my dear little children and my love to you my dear wife your husband,

John W. Brendel

Written to:
Mrs. Ann M. Brendel
West Newton, Westmorland County, Penna.

Camp 11 Regt. PV. Near Rapidan River
October 11, 1863

Dear Wife:

I received your kind letter of the 2nd and was very glad to hear from you and feel very thankful to God that our health is as good as it is. I just feel middling not like I used to feel. I feel as if I was 50 or 60 years old and this kind of living would make anybody feel old. We're out on picket more than half of our time. The picket lines are so close together we can talk to other side but it is not allowed for to talk to them anymore. Our boys traded paper with them at first when we came here but it is not allowed now at all to have any communication with them. I will be at home this fall sometime if God spares my life and health. There was an order read on dress parade last evening we can go home and fill up our regiment and go for three years and get four- hundred two dollars in the time we have to stay goes in, *but I don't know whether the regiment will go or not. I may take the four-hundred two dollars and stay three years more and we get one-hundred dollar bounty for what we have served which will make five-hundred two dollars. If we take it well will all be at home this winter recruiting. I want you to tell me who said it was a disgrace to be a soldier. You must excuse me for not writing more to you at present. I have to get ready for picket. We came off the day before yesterday and have to go out today. We will be out two days. Now dear Annie I want you to write as soon as this comes to hand. I think sometimes you are long about writing for there is nothing in the world does me so much good as to hear from you good bye. May almighty God bless you and my little children and take care of you all and spare me to get home. Your affectionate husband,*

John W. Brendel

Written to:
No envelope

Camp 11th Regt. Thoroughfare Gap
October 22, 1863

Dear Wife:

After my love to you and my dear little children I will inform you that I am still living but not very well but I hope to God that these few lines may find you enjoying good health and that will make me feel a great deal better. Lawyer is sick and sent back to Washington Hospital. Will is well, we left the Rapidan River on the 10th and have been on the march ever since. We have been marching day and night nearly every hour since we started. I received two letters from you since I left the Rapidan. We only got one mail since we left there and that was the 19th and I was very glad to hear from you for I thought it long to hear from you. I want you to write often for when the army is moving I have not much chance to write to you. I think if God spares my life and health that I will be at home before long. We will be paid next month I think. I will come home pretty soon after that. We came through Thoroughfare Gap night before last. You have to excuse me for not writing more to you for I am very tired and don't feel like doing anything. But I have my duty to do no difference how tired I am. No more at present, your affectionate husband,

John W. Brendel

Write soon and often good evening.

Written to:
No envelope

Camp 11th Regt. Bristow Station Virginia
November 1, 1863

Dear Wife:

I feel very thankful to God that I am spared this Sunday morning to sit down and answer your kind and long looked for letter. I feel very thankful to God that you are all well and hope these few lines may find you enjoying the same blessing. We have had some hard marching since we left the Rapidan. We have had no regular fight since we left Geddisburg [sic]. We don't call little skirmishes, fights, them was just little brushes to make the Rebs get up and dust themselves. I have not heard from Lawyer for some time, Will is well. I will be at home as soon as I can if God spares my health and life and I trust in him for he has always brought me through safe this far and I trust God will spare us to meet once more on Earth. We was mustered in yesterday for our pay and I suppose we will get it in about ten or fifteen days. No more at present my dear wife but my love to you and children. May God bless us all now and forever. Write a little more regular than you do. I have told you often when we was on a march we could not write when we pleased just when we can. I am very sorry to hear that you are strapped but I have no money to send you now but I expect to get some before long. Your affectionate husband,

John W. Brendel

Write soon.

The most common type of religion during the Civil War was Evangelical Protestant Christianity. Many soldiers on both sides maintained a personal faith despite the death and destruction that surrounded them. One reason for their beliefs was noted as gratitude to God that they had survived battles. Others believed their comrades experienced peace and happiness in their dying moments.

Most Union regiments possessed a chaplain. Most, but not all, were well qualified. Many chaplains went into battle walking only a few paces behind the ranks and were often the first to render aid to a wounded soldier.[38]

Written to:
Mrs. Ann M. Brendel
West Newton, Westmorland County, Penna.

Camp 11th Regt. PV Liberty Virginia
near Bealeton Station
November 19, 1863

Dear Wife:

I received yours of the 10th and was glad to hear from you. I just came in off picket and don't feel like writing but thank God I feel pretty well. I was sick for four or five days but feel pretty well again. I hope these few lines may find you enjoying good health. I drawed my money yesterday. I will send you some as soon as I can get a chance to send it. It is a little dangerous to send it at the present time the guerrillas are thick here now. There has been a good many of our soldiers shot by them since we came back here. You must excuse me for not writing more. I will try and write you a good letter the next time. I would have sent you some money in this letter but I was afraid you would not get it. Have to quit and go on inspection. Your true and affectionate husband,

John W. Brendel

Try and write a little more regular than you do and once a week at least if you love me.

The previous letter was written on the same day that President Lincoln delivered the Gettysburg Address in which he dedicated the Gettysburg National Cemetery.

From November 26 thru December 2, the Army of the Potomac advanced south across the Rapidan River to engage the Confederates at Mine Run, Virginia. Once there, they found the Confederates to be well fortified.

After two engagements, Meade realized any further attacks would fail.[39] The weather was also very cold which also hindered military operations. The army returned north of the Rappahannock River and went into winter quarters. During the Mine Run Expedition, the 11th Pennsylvania served primarily as a rear guard.[40]

Written to:
No envelope

Camp 11th Regt. Kelly's Ford
December the 12th, 1863

Dear Wife:

I received your kind letter and was glad to hear from you that you was getting better again. I hope you will be well again when I get home. I have not been well since we came off that last march. We had a pretty hard time of it. We really froze and starved to death. We have been fixing up winter quarters and I have not time to write much at present but will write to you soon again. Give my respects to Mr. Davidson and tell him I will write to him soon. I sent you five dollars in the other letter I sent you and you will find five more in this. I had no chance to send you money yet from here. I will be at home as soon as I can. I have made you and Jenny a ring a piece but I will not send them in this on account of the money being in this letter. But I will send them in the next. No more at present may God take care of us all. Your affectionate husband,

John W. Brendel

We got no mail since we started on this last till the other day here. You must write soon as this comes to hand for I think it long to hear from you.

Written to:
No envelope

> Camp 11th Regt. PV. Near Kelly's Ford
> Dec. the 22, 1863

Dear Wife:

I received your letter yesterday and was glad to hear from you but was sorry to hear that you had all been sick. I have been sick every since we took that last hard march and do not feel much better today. I will be at home before long. They are giving furloughs now and as soon as it comes my turn I will start for home and that will be soon. The captain is at home now. I sent you fifteen dollars in a different letter. Five in each one and you will find two rings in this one for you and one for Jenny. Hers is bone and yours is purcha?[sic] I made them while on picket facing the enemy. So you can keep them as a memorial of your husbands love and Jenny's as a fathers love to her and I will bring something along with me when I come for Bobby. So I think you had better stay at home in about three weeks. No more at present but remain your affectionate husband. You must excuse my scribbling and write as soon as this comes to hand for I am not fit to write at present,

John W. Brendel

I have a fifteen dollar ring on my finger that I drawed in the New York lottery that I will bring home with me when I come home.

Written to:
Mrs. Ann M. Brendel
Westnewton. Westmoreland Co. Penna.

Camp 11th Regt. near Culpeper, Va.
December the 30th, 1863

Dear Wife:

I sit down to drop you a few lines to let you know how I am getting along. I am not well at all but thank God I am better. I am able to be about. I have wrote you two letters since I got one from you and think it very long to hear from you. I think the whole regiment will be at home next month. They are going back to recruit up again and we will get a furlough for thirty-five days at least if not more. So I think you can look for me at home next month. We had our winter quarters fired up at Kelly's Ford and are here now. I sent you fifteen dollars to you by mail in three different letters and have not heard whether you got it or not. Tomorrow we will be mustered for two months more and will be paid in a few days. The payrolls are made out now. I will write to you as soon as I get a letter from you. I'll not write any more tonight as I hope to God that I will soon be at home and we can talk face to face that our joys may be new dear Anna. I was very glad to hear that you was getting better. This is the third letter I wrote since I got one from you. I want you to write as soon as you get this letter for I think it very long to hear from *you but I hope we will meet earlong [sic]. The captain is at home yet on a furlough. Good night my wife I hope God will permit us to meet earlong [sic] no more. But may God bless us now and for ever. Your affectionate husband,*

John W. Brendel

I sent you and Jenny a ring a piece in the last letter. I wrote to you for a Christmas gift and have not heard whether you got them or not. I made them both myself for a memorial of old Virg.

The year 1863, ended similar to the way it began. Both armies were on in camp on Virginia soil hoping the next year would be their last as soldiers. The past year had certainly hardened Brendel as a soldier. He experienced the monotony of camp life and survived extreme weather conditions. While he was quite ill like many of his comrades, he managed to avoid bullets and shells at the Battles of Fredericksburg, Chancellorsville and Gettysburg.

Post office - Falmouth, Virginia
Group in front of post office tent at Army of the Potomac Headquarters. LOC

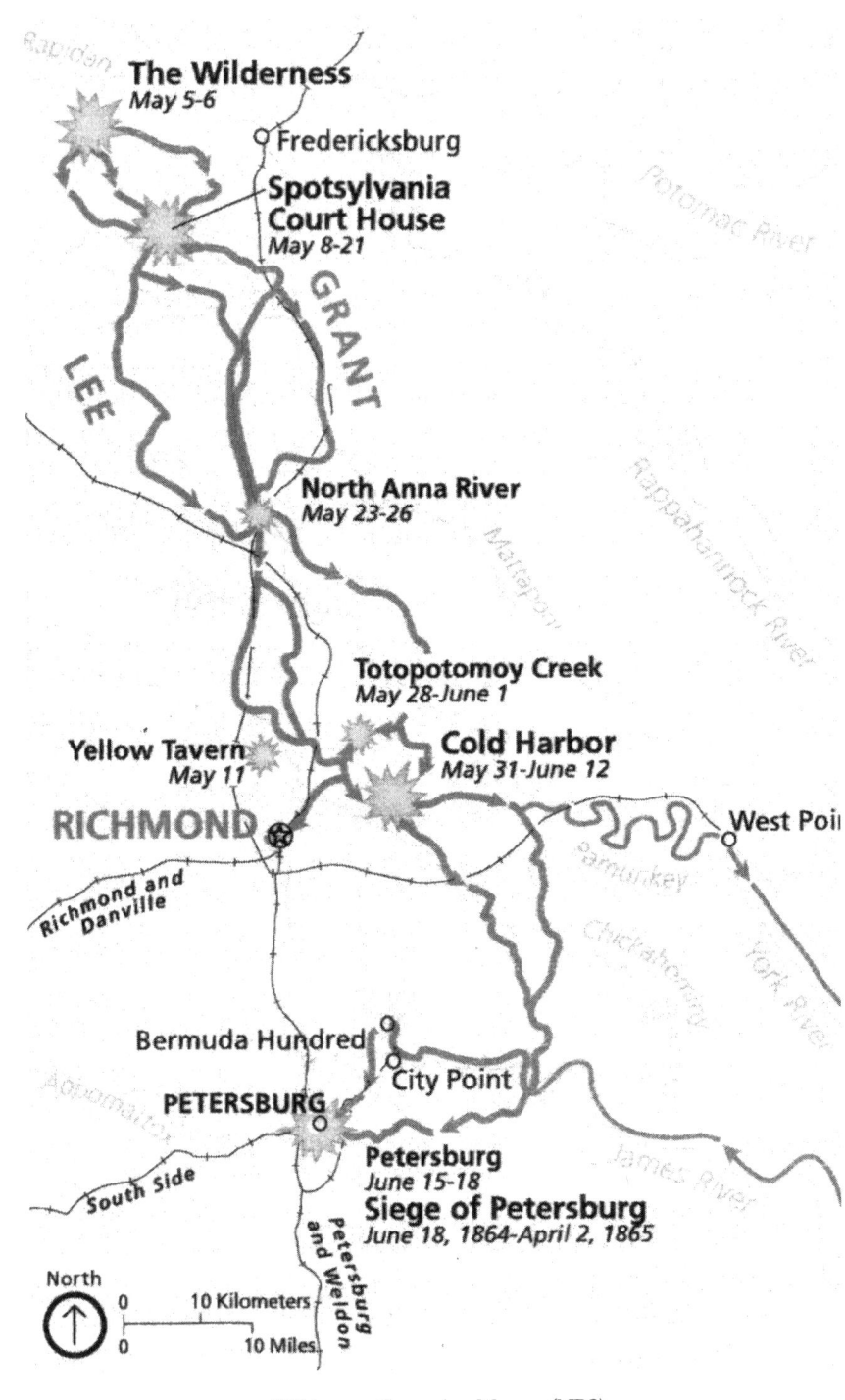

Wilderness Campaign Map (NPS)

Chapter 3

1864 - May God Bless Us All

Many people thought that by 1864 the war would be over. Instead, the armies were in winter quarters awaiting another year of combat and bloodshed with no end to hostilities in sight.

Written to:
Mrs. Ann M. Brendel
Westnewton, Westmoreland Co. Penna.
*Soldiers Letter- Due 3 Cents

Camp 11th Regt. Cedar Mountain Va.
January 14th, 1864

Dear Wife:

I sit down to answer your long looked for letter and feel very glad to hear from you that you are all getting better. Though I have not been well myself for some time I have been taking med-

icine for sometime myself but feel little better than I did. I sent you fifteen dollars in three letters. Five in each and thought I would never get an answer. I think we will soon be back to Harrisburg. The captain is there now to see about going back and as soon as he gets back I will write to you and let you know all about it. The whole regiment is going back to Washington but I can't tell how soon they will get off but I think it will be before long. We have not been paid off yet but think we will be paid in a few days. I think I will wear this ring myself till I come home and maybe you will have some of them other ones at home till I come. If I was to send it you would only give it to someone else to wear and so I think I had better wear it myself. It is a very nice ring. I would have wrote sooner But I was looking for a letter from you every time. The mail came but looked in vain and thought if you did not write to me I would to you. We have put up winter quarters here and live tolerably comfortable. We have had some very cold winter weather here. There was one man in Co. C froze to death the night we came here. His name is Curry. He belongs to the same company that Will does. We have had a good deal of snow. It is pleasant here today but I think we will have more snow. I must bring my letter to a close. We are fixing our little house. My love to you my dear wife and children. I think we will be home before long. We can't tell when we can get off we must just go when we get the chance. Write soon, no more at present but remain your affectionate husband,

John W. Brendel

The soldier that froze to death was George W. Curry. Curry enlisted on September 9, 1861. He was wounded at Antietam and Gettysburg. He died on January 2, 1864.

Written to:
No envelope

>Camp 11th Regt. PV. Cedar Mountain
>January the 24, 64

My Dear Wife:

I received your kind and welcome letter last night the 23rd and you can't tell how glad I was to hear from you once more for I thought I would never hear from you anymore. For I had only got one letter from you this year and this one last night is two and you can't tell how sorry I felt to hear that you are no better yet. But I have a hope that God will take care of you put your trust in him. I have been sick for some time myself. I have not been on duty since we came to this camp. I feel a little better today than I have for sometime. I have not been bedfast but you know I must be very sick when I take my bed. I think I will get home the first of next month. I was just talking to the adjunct a few minutes ago and he said our regiment will go back to Washington the first of next month. We can't get home until the regiment goes back. That is what we are waiting on or we would have been at home before this. We have not been paid off yet. We was to have been paid off by the 15th and this is Sunday the 24th. But if we are not paid before we start back we will be paid in Washington. There has been none of our company sworn in yet. The balance of the regiment has been sworn in for three years but we will re-enlist when we go back to Washington. I sent you fifteen dollars in three different letters, five in each one. I think it was before I sent you the ring. I have the other nice ring yet and think I will keep it until I come myself. The Johnny Rebs sent in a flag of truce four days ago and give us twenty-four hours to leave but we are still here yet. There is still some of them come into our lines and gives themselves up. There was twelve Negroes come into our lines last night and they said the Rebs are falling back but we can't place much confidence in Negroes. My dear wife you must excuse these few scribble lines as I am a poor hand to write when I am not well. I hope I will be at home in a few days or weeks at least and then we can have one of them old fashion talks. Then I can tell you more than I could write. Write me a few lines occasionally for you can't tell how disappointed I feel night after night when the mail comes in and no letter for me. No more at present but remain your true and faithful husband. May God protect us now and forever,

John W. Brendel

I nearly forgot to give my love to my dear children and tell them to be good children. Tell them that pappy loves them and that he will be at home in a few weeks if God spares his life and health. Kiss the children for me and think of me while you are kissing them.

Written to:
Mrs. Anne M. Brendel
Westnewton, Westmoreland Co. Penna.
*Soldiers Letter- Due 6 Cents

> Camp 11th Regt. PV. Culpeper,
> Culpeper Co., Va.
> February the 1st, 1864

Dear Wife:

I received your kind letter dated Jan. 25th. You can't tell how glad I was to hear from you but I felt so sorry to hear that you was getting no better yet. Though I am not well myself nor have not been for sometime. But I have a hope in God that he will permit us to meet before long. We left Cedar Mountain and came back to Culpeper, the county seat of Culpeper. We came back here day before yesterday and look every day for transportation back to Washington and then I think I will be pretty soon at home and I can tell you more than I am able to write at present. We have not been paid off yet but will be in a few days. Our regiment have got their quarters in a big three story brick. My dear wife you must excuse me for not writing more to you at present but I don't feel like writing. But I hope the time will be short till we see each other and talk face-to-face and our joy may be new. May God protect us now and forever,

John W. Brendel

Write soon. I think we will get off this week. They say we will get off on Wednesday but we are so often disappointed that I never believe anything till I see it.

On February 2, the re-enlisted men of the 11th Pennsylvania were granted a thirty-five day furlough to go home and recruit more soldiers.[1]

Written to:
Mrs. Ann M. Brendel
Westnewton, Westmoreland Co. Penna.

Soldiers Rest, Alexandria
Feb. 6, 1864

Dear Wife:

I have nothing much to write to you at present. We left Culpeper yesterday and got here today at dinner. Expected to be in Washington last night but we had a collision. A locomotive run into our train last night and smashed two cars all to pieces and wounded six or seven men, none very dangerous and another broke through to long bridge and we can't go until they get the bridge repaired. You need not write to me until you hear from me. For I think we will be at home in two or three days. I am not well at all and expect you are not either. But I hope we will both be better till I get home. My love to you my dear wife. No more at present, but remain your affectionate husband,

John W. Brendel

Recruiting stations were established in Pittsburg [sic], Greensburg, Lock Haven, Jersey Shore and Mauch Chunk (known today as Jim Thorpe). On March 20, the regiment reformed in Harrisburg and from there proceeded to Washington, arriving on March 28. While at home, the regiment of two hundred seventy six men recruited three-hundred fourteen additional soldiers.[2]

While the 11th Pennsylvania was on furlough, major changes were taking place in Washington. On March 3, Ulysses S. Grant, the successful commander in the western theater of the Civil War, was summoned to Washington for a commission as the newly re-instituted position of lieutenant-general. The commission placed Grant in charge of all United States armies. While General Meade remained in command of the Army of the Potomac, Grant was now the military boss.[3]

With Grants arrival, the command structure within the Army of the Potomac was consolidated into three Corps: Maj. General Winfield S. Hancock commanded the Second Corps; Maj. General Gouverneur K. Warren commanded the Fifth Corps; and Maj. General John Sedgwick commanded the Sixth Corps.

The 11th Pennsylvania was assigned to the Fifth Corps, Second Division, commanded by Brig. General John C. Robinson, Second Brigade commanded by Brig. General Henry Baxter.[4]

Written to:
No envelope

Alexandria
March 31, 64

Dear Wife:

You must excuse me for not writing but I was not able to write. I feel a great deal better this morning and hope to God you are well for that's all my trouble. I did not get paid yet but as soon as I get paid I will send you the money. Tell Mr. Plummer he shall get his money as soon as we get paid. Write as soon as this comes to hand. In the next letter I will give you all the particulars. No more at present but remain your true and faithful husband,

John W. Brendel

Written to:
Mrs. Ann M. Brendel
West Newton, Westmorland County, Penna.

Camp near Culpeper
April 4, 1864

Dear Wife,

I take my pen in hand to drop you a few lines to let you know how I am getting along. Thank God that I am a great deal better than I was when I was at home. I pray to God that these few lines may find you and the children in good health for I felt so bad when I was at home that I expect you had a sorrowful time with me when I was at home. But you must excuse me for being so ill-natured when I was at home for I felt so bad that I hardly knew what I was doing. When I started from home I had allowed to be back but I was so bad that I did not get down to see little Sammy but I sent him one dollar by your father. The regiment started for Harrisburg and I got on the train and I went along and was not able to write to you till we got to Alexandria and there I dropped you a few lines. I don't know whether you could read them or not. I did not get my money yet but as soon as I get it, I will send you as much as will pay off all the debts you owe, and some for you to live on too. I have fifty-two dollars coming to me now and I think that will square you up and have some left. You will have to borrow some money to do you till I am paid. We was to get our money in Pittsburg and then in Harrisburg and then in Washington and then in Alexandra and have not got it yet and so they will have to wait till I get the money and they shall have what is coming to them. You need not send them things to me I drawed other ones since. You can take the shirt and make baby something out of it and the drawers and socks, use them for anything you can. The oil cloth will make you a cover for your kitchen table. My dear Annie you said you thought I did not love you. But my dear child I love you with my whole heart. God knows that I love you and I hope you love me too. The mail is starting out and I must quit. I trust God will permit us to meet again. Pardon me for the wrongs I have done. Good- bye, a kiss for you and the dear little children. May almighty God bless and preserve us forever. Your true and lonely husband.

John W. Brendel

Direct your letters as usual. Write as soon as this comes to hand for I think so long to hear from you. We have had very rough weather since I left. It's raining and snowing now. Give me all the particulars.

With both armies located between Washington and Richmond, they held the same relative positions as when the war began. Grant's general plan was to concentrate all of his forces against the Confederate army. In a letter dated April 4, Grant instructed Meade: "Wherever Lee goes, there you will go also".[5] The overall goal of the Overland Campaign was to defeat Lee's Confederate army and capture the Confederate capitol: Richmond.

Written to:
No envelope

Camp near Culpeper, VA
April 25, 1864

My Dear Wife,

I was just writing a few lines to my mother (ed. mother's name is Susan) and I thought perhaps you would want to write a few words to her. So I will direct it to you and you can put it in an envelop and direct it to mother in care of Jacob S. Ross. Dear Anna I wrote you such a nice letter last Sunday a week ago and have got no answer from you a week ago yet. So I will not write till I get an answer from you. I sent you two dollars in the last letter. You can read mother's letter and that will do you as much good as if I had wrote it to you. As soon as we get paid I will send you plenty of money. No more my dear wife, may the blessing of God rest with you now and forever Amen. Your affectionate husband,

John W. Brendel

Write soon.

Written to:
Miss. Jeny Brendel
West Newton, Westmorland County, Penna.
* Soldiers Letter

Camp 11th Regt. PVT,
Culpeper, VA
April 29, 1864

Dear daughter,

I received your kind little letter and was very glad to hear from you and you can't tell how proud I felt to think that I had a daughter that could write me such a nice letter. I think the war will be over this fall and I will come home and stay with you and Musy [sic] and baby. Give my love to Musy [sic] and baby and to poor Sam too. Tell them to be good boys and I expect you to be a good girl too. For you must set them the example for you are the oldest and as the old cock crows so the young ones learn. You must excuse my scribbling for I expect you can hardly read this letter but you must get Musy [sic] to help you to read it for I am a awkward writer. Anyhow we have a big company now. We have sixty-four men present and about ninety in all, makes a pretty large company. Goodbye Jeny, write soon, be a good girl *till I see you again and I hope that will be before long. No more at present but remain your affectionate father,*

John W. Brendel

Written to:
Mrs. Ann M. Brendel
Westnewton, Westmoreland Co. Penna.

> Camp 11th Regt. near Culpeper, Va.
> April 29, 1864

Dear Wife:

I received your kind and welcomed letter the 28th instant and was very glad to hear from you and to hear that you was all in reasonable health. I feel first rate myself only my back and it is not better yet. But I thank God that we are as well as we are. The army is generally in good health with the exception of the mumps. The weather is fine and pleasant, nothing strange going on here. General Burnside's is at Manassas Junction about twenty miles from here with forty-thousand troops, eight-thousand of which are colored troops. You said you wanted to write to your brother. You direct the same as to me only he belongs to Company C. You said in your last letter that some of the folks in Westnewton said that I was paid off in Pittsburg. You can tell them that they are liars and the truth is not in them and they had better pay off their own debts and attend to their own business and by so doing they will get bitch. Give my love to Sarah Shaffer. You can tell her that her brother John is in the Penitentiary in Allegheny. I would have went to see him but I under stood no person can get in anymore to see the inmates. I suppose we will be paid in a few days. They are making out the pay rolls now. I sent a letter to you to send to mother. I thought you might like to write some in it too. My love to you and the children. Tell my dear little daughter that I was much pleased to get a letter from her. Tell her that she must write again. If you think you ought to tell Sarah where her brother is do *so for it is true. I saw McSwain and said he was put in for stealing a horse. I wrote Mr. Plummer a few lines but you can tell him that he shall have his money as soon as I am paid and I think that will be soon. Write soon and often for you know I have not the chance to write you when we are on a move. No more at present but may God bless us all. Your Affectionate husband,*

John W. Brendel

President Lincoln authorized the enlistment of African-American troops in January 1863. African-American troops were gradually accepted by white soldiers, but not as equals. At first, African-American soldiers performed menial tasks such as digging ditches and latrines. Eventually, African-American soldiers gained acceptance and a measure of respect. By the end of the war, twenty-one African-American soldiers had earned the newly created Congressional Medal of Honor.[6]

On May 3 and 4, the Army of the Potomac moved south to engage the enemy. The soldiers had three days rations in their haversacks and fifty rounds of cartridges in their cartridge boxes.[7] The Union army encountered the Confederates in a heavily wooded area located west of Chancellorsville in an area know as the Wilderness.

The battle raged for two days: May 5 - 6. The 11th Pennsylvania became engaged in the fight later in the day of the 5th with Wadsworth's Fourth brigade. The battle, fought in thick forest terrain, roared for hours. Soldiers fired blindly into the seeming invisible Confederates in the dark forest.

On May 6, the 11th Pennsylvania was heavily engaged. Baxter's Second Brigade, of which the 11th Pennsylvania was a part of, was badly shredded. During the fight, Baxter was severely wounded. A rifle ball passed through his leg, killing his horse.[8] Command of the brigade fell to Col. Coulter. After three days of fighting the ranks had thinned terribly. These factors led to the Second Brigade being transferred to Brig. General Samuel Crawford's Third Division.

After battle at the Wilderness, Grant did not retreat and rest. Instead, he advanced the army southeast towards Spotsylvania Court House. These actions resulted in pressure being placed on the Confederates.

The Army of the Potomac fought a series of engagements from May 8 to May 21 in Spotsylvania County. On May 10, the Fifth and Sixth Corps made a general assault upon the enemy at Laurel Hill. The 11th Pennsylvania advanced within one hundred yards of enemy entrenchments and held the position until relieved for five hours. The brigade suffered two-hundred twenty nine casualties.[9] In a message to Chief of Staff Halleck, Grant proposed to fight it out on this line if it took all summer.

Other actions taking place during this time included: Corbin's Bridge (May 8); Ny River (May 9); Po River and Bloody Angle (May 10); Salient or Bloody Angle (May 12-13); Piney Branch Church (May 15); Harrison House (May18); and Harris Farm (May19).[10]

Undeterred by heavy losses, Grant continued the offensive towards the North Anna River.

Written to:
Mrs. Anne M. Brendel
Westnewton, Westmoreland Co. Penna.

May 18th,1864

Dear Wife:

Thank God I am still living yet and hope you are all living and well. The fighting commenced on the 5th and is still going on yet. I have been in eight or nine fights since this commenced. The mail is in just now and I got a letter from J.S.Ross and one from Ell and you can't tell how bad I was disappointed when I did not get one from you. I thought it could not be possible that

I did not get one from you. Try for Gods sake and write. We are lying in line of battle now looking every minute for another fight. No more, I hope God will bring me through safe as always so far.

John W. Brendel

The Second Corps crossed the North Anna River at Jericho Mills, advanced southeast, and engaged the Confederates on May 23. On May 24, the Union's attack went up against a well entrenched Confederate line. Lee formed his battle lines in an inverted V formation.

The Fifth Corps was up against A. P. Hill's Corps.[11] In the end, Grant ordered the Union army to retreat back across the North Anna River. Undeterred by this setback, Grant continued his offensive easterly towards Cold Harbor.

Written to:
Mrs. Ann M. Brendel
Westnewton, Westmoreland Co. Penna.

Camp 11th Regt. PV.
Richmond 9 miles
June the 4th, 1864

Dear Wife:

Thank God I am well with the exception of my back. I received your kind letter and was very glad to hear from you. Just came in off the skirmish line. Seven killed and several wounded out of our company. Will is well. We are in the breastworks now. We have had very hard fighting for one month today. I am sorry we did not get paid yet and I can't send any money. But it will be the more when it comes and that will be as soon as I can get it. So you will have to shift the best you can till it comes. My dear wife I put my trust in God and he is able to take care if me and you too. No more, may God take care of us till we meet again. Not much time for writing now. Give my respects to George

Plummer and tell him I wrote him a letter and got no answer yet. Give my respects to all inquiring friends and my love to you and family. Write as soon as this comes to hand. Your affectionate husband,

John W. Brendel

....

After three days of sparring for control of the crossroads near Cold Harbor, Grant commenced a general assault on June 3. At the Battle of Cold Harbor, the Union Fifth Corps suffered heavy losses along the skirmish line in the vicinity of Bethesda Church. Grant commented in his memoirs "I have always regretted that the last assault at Cold Harbor was ever made".[12]

In order to isolate Richmond, General Grant needed to cut off supplies. Due to its five railroads, Petersburg was the main supply route for Richmond and the Army of Northern Virginia. Grant's problem was that fortifications were started in 1862 to hamper any approach of the Union army from the north. Breastworks and artillery emplacements stretched for ten miles in a semi-circle east of the city. On June 12, Grant began moving the Army of the Potomac south from the James River to the well protected city of Petersburg. The Union would lay siege to Petersburg until April 1865.[13]

During the early years of the Civil War, most battles were fought with soldiers standing upright facing one another. However, by the summer of 1864, the armies in the eastern theatre of war resorted to siege operations.

A component of siege operations was the construction of breastworks. Breastworks were barriers constructed of earth and wood designed to protect defenders. Incorporated on the earth-works were cut trees sharpened on one end facing the enemy (abatis). When possible, a deep ditch was dug in front of the breastworks.[14]

Written to:
Mrs. Ann M. Brendel
Westnewton, Westmoreland Co. Penna.
*Soldiers Letter- Due 3 Cents

Camp near Petersburg Va.
July 4, 1864

Dear Wife:

I received your kind and welcomed letter which gave me great pleasure to hear from you that you was all well and thank God I am enjoying pretty good health myself. It is pretty quiet along the line today. There is but little firing along the line today. This is twice I spent the 4th of July in the line of battle and I hope to God it may be the last, for I am getting tired of this way of living. I would like to be at home today. I think I could enjoy myself a great deal better than here. But I hope and pray to God that there will be peace before another 4th comes. My dear wife I have no money to send you but you will have to shift the best you can till I get my pay and then I think we can get along for a few days. I have eighty-eight dollars coming to me now and I am beginning to get down on the present administration. They are pretty strict with the soldiers but it appears to me as if they did not care when they paid them. The regulations of war calls for the soldier to be paid every two months. I have had no tobacco for nearly two months, only what I begged and if I had thought the government would have made a beggar out of me I never would have gone into the service. But here I am and I will have to stick it out. The picket lines are so close together we can talk to them. Some of the boys trade coffee and sugar for tobacco but I don't have no dealings with them. Our whole army has strong breast-works up and are pretty well fortified. Tell Mr. Leighty to send me a half-pound tobacco by mail and you can pay him as soon as I get paid and I hope that will be before long and he will confer a great favor. You can read this for him and if he sends it is right and if not it is still right. There is no strange news to write. The army news you have as soon as we. No more at present my dear wife but my sincere prayers that this cursed rebellion be crushed out and we all get home in peace. My dear wife write soon for I think it long to hear from you. Will is well. My love to you and family. May God protect us now and forever.

Your affectionate husband,

John W. Brendel

On July 4, 1863, Brendel was still on the battlefield at Gettysburg. On this July 4th he was laying in a trench at Petersburg.

Written to:
Mrs. Ann M. Brendel
Westnewton., Westmoreland Co. Penna.
*Soldiers Letter - Due 3 Cents

Camp near Petersburg Va.
Sunday July 31, 1864

Dear Wife:

I take my pen in hand to drop you a few lines to let you know that I received your kind and welcome letter and was thankful to God that you was all well though I am not well myself. But feel thankful that I am as well as I am. I have a very bad cough and pain on my breast. We had a hard fight on our right yesterday. I can't give you the facts for there are so many reports that we can't believe any without knowing them to be true. Blowed up one of the Reb forts and took one line of their breast-works and I understand they have took them back again lost a great many men on both sides. You will have the news before this reaches you. William is well, the last I heard of Lawyer he was in the invalid corps. The Christian Commission has been very good to us. They have sent us a heap of nice things such as; canned fruit, potatoes, chicken, pickles, sauerkraut, red beats, and cabbage. I don't know what we would have done for paper and envelopes if it had not been for them. The weather is very dry and warm. We have had no rain of any amount this summer. We dig wells to get our water. It is much better than the spring water. The health of the army is as good as can be expected. I have nothing of particular to write. If I was at home I could tell you a heap of things with pleasure. My dear wife you will have to do the best you can till I get paid. I have over one-hundred dollars coming to me now and I do hope and pray that I may get it before long. For it bothers my mind a great deal to hear that you are in want for money. May God take care of us all till we meet again. Give my respects to all inquiring friends. I will not write until you answer this. My love to you and family my dear Anna. Your husband,

John W. Brendel

Excuse my poor letter for I don't feel much like writing.

The blown up fort that Brendel referred to in the previous letter would become known as the Battle of the Crater. The 48th Pennsylvania of the Ninth Corps was comprised of miners from northeastern Pennsylvania. These miners devised a plan to tunnel a mine under the Confederate fortifications, pack it with explosives, and blow it up. Work started on June 15 and was completed by July 30.

At 4:45 a.m. on July 30, the explosives were detonated. The hole created by the blast was 30 feet deep, 60 to 80 feet wide and 170 feet long. The explosion killed 278 Confederates and destroyed two guns of the battery.

Following the explosion, soldiers of the Ninth Corps advanced but were not prepared to descend into such a deep hole or ascend up the other end. This challenge afforded the Confederates time to regroup and defend the position.[15] While the concept of blowing up the fortification was a good one, in the end it served as a terrible debacle for the Union forces.

Written to:
Mrs. Anna M. Brendel
Westnewton, Westmoreland Co. Penna.

Camp near Petersburg, Va.
August 10th, 1864

Dear Wife:

I take my pen in hand to drop you a few lines to let you know that I received your two kind letters and one from Ell Brendel and the two likenesses and was glad to hear that you was in tolerable good health though I am not very good myself. I have a bad cough and a pain on my breast. Blistered (ed. cupped) but has not helped me much yet. But I still feel thankful to God for his goodness towards us in sparing our unprofitable lives through these many difficulties and hope is through the mercy of God I will get through safe and we will meet once more on earth that our joys may be full. My dear Anna I have confidence in God that he will bring me safe through if I put my trust in him. Give my love to my dear little children and kiss them for me and tell them pappy sent them that kiss and he said they must be good children till I get home and I hope that will be before very long. Well Anna I did not get any money yet but I hope I will get it before long, have been looking for the paymaster every day. A good part of the army has been paid. We had a fine rain here last night. It is just as warm here today as ever, no more at present. The war news you get in the papers are corrector than I could write to you. Give my respects to all inquiring friends and in particular to Plummer and Leighty. Let me know if Ios Werrick [sic] got home or not. I will send you some money as soon as I get paid. Tell Jenny and Robby I will try and send them some too. I will write to Ell as soon as I get some paper. My love to you my dear wife. Write soon and often. Your affectionate husband,

John W. Brendel

Written to:
Mrs. Anne Brendel
Westnewton, Westmoreland Co. Penna.

> Camp 11th Regt. PV
> Near Petersburg Va.
> August 14, 1864

Dear Wife:

I take my pen in hand to let you know that I received your kind letter with Jenny's and Bobby's Photograph and feel thankful to God that you was well but I am not well myself. But thank God I am no worse. I was paid six months on the 12th but have had no chance to express the money yet on the account of the explosion at City Point last week. There was a large load of ammunition blown up and blowed up the express office, but it will be open again on Tuesday and then I will express about sixty-five dollars more to you. Dr. Ausburn told me he would go to City Point and express the money for me. It is seven or eight miles from here. Enclosed you will find five dollars. I would send more but I am afraid you might not get it and money is hard earned here to loose it if it can be helped. This is Sunday, all quiet along the line. No firing just now, there was a little this morning on our right. I will write as soon as I send you the money. Write as soon as this comes to hand for I am always very anxious to hear from you and my dear little pets. I would like to be with you but my calling is here and I must obey. But my prayer is that the day is not far distant when we can lay down our arms and have peace once more. Give my respects to Mr. Lighty and Mr. Plummer and all inquiring friends. No more at present but excuse my bad writing for I am not in writing order. I have a little touch of the toothache and I suppose that you know a body don't feel much like writing then. May God watch over us and take care of us now and forever, is your affectionate husband's sincere prayer.

John W. Brendel

City Point, located at the junction of the James and Appomattox Rivers, was a major seaport for the arrival of Union supplies. During the last ten months of the war, it served as the headquarters for General Grant. On August 9, 1864 a Rebel saboteur detonated a time bomb (twelve pounds of explosives packed in a candle box with a percussion cap and clockwork mechanism) on an ammunition barge. The ammunition barge was loaded with twenty to thirty thousand artillery rounds and more than seventy-five thousand rounds of small-arms ammunition. The huge explosion killed or wounded over 300 people and destroyed over two-million dollars worth of property. General Grant narrowly escaped injury.[16]

Written to:
Mrs. Anna M. Brendel
Westnewton, Westmoreland Co. Penna.

Camp 11th Regt. PV.
near Petersburg Va.
August 17

Dear Wife:

After my love to you and family I hope these few lines will find you in good health though I am not much better myself. I sent you sixty-five dollars yesterday by express and five a few days ago by mail which you will receive before you get this. Let me hear from you as soon as this comes to hand for I will be uneasy till I hear if you got the money. For it would be a hard stroke to loose seventy dollars now. Pay Mr. Leighty for that tobacco. It has been very wet here for a few days. I will have to quit for the mail is ready to start out and a big rain is coming. I will write you more in a day or two. I have not time to write. We are packed up to move. I must quit,

John W. Brendel

By now, it was evident to Grant that attacking the Confederate fortifications head on was out of the question. Grant needed to stretch the Confederate lines and keep Lee off balance. It was vital that Lee's supply line be cut off. In addition, Lee was sending troops to the Shenandoah in support of Maj. General Early. Grant wanted those soldiers to remain in defense of Richmond.

On August 18, Warren's Fifth Corps seized the Weldon Railroad at Globe Tavern. The 11th Pennsylvania advanced with the Third Division, Second Brigade north towards Petersburg. There, the skirmishers soon became engaged with the enemy. The 11th Pennsylvania was positioned on the right. Confederate General Beauregard sent General Heth to stop the attack.[17]

By evening, the 11th Pennsylvania was erecting breastworks, which would become a permanent extension of the siege lines. On the afternoon of the 19th, the Confederates broke through the line capturing some of the Yankees. The majority of the losses in the 11th Pennsylvania fell upon companies D, E and Brendel's Company G.[18]

Written to:
Miss Jennie Brinddell
Care of Mrs. A. M. Brindell
West-Newton, Westmoreland County, Penna.

11th Regt. near Petersburg
August the 26th, 1864

Dear Daughter:

I take my pen in hand to write you a few lines to let you know I am well and hope these few lines may find you all enjoying the same blessing. I found a nice letter handkerchief and thought I would send it to you. It would be nice to go to church with and when you would look at it you would think of me. Tell mother I received a letter from her stating she got the money. I sent her five dollars by mail and sixty-five dollars by express, makes seventy dollars all. Dear Jennie I have not much time to write to you at present. We are lying in line of battle and don't know what time we may be attacked. But you be a good girl and pray for pappy that he may get home safe once more to see you all. No more but give my love to mother and Robbie. Tell Mus I wrote to her yesterday and I won't write until I get answer. Your affectionate father,

W. Brendel

Written to:
Mrs. Ann M. Brendel
Westnewton, Westmoreland Co. Penna.

Camp 11th Regt.
6 miles south of Petersburg
Weldon Railroad, Va.
September the 2, 1864

My Dear Anny:

I received your kind and welcomed letter dated Aug. 25th which gave me great pleasure to hear that you was all well and feel very thankful to God for his goodness towards us for sparing our unprofitable lives through so many difficulties. I was very glad to hear that you got the seventy dollars that I sent you, for I expect you needed it. There is thirty-six dollars coming to me now and I expect I will be paid off in about ten or twelve days. We was mustered for pay, day before yesterday. I wrote Jennie a nice letter and sent her a nice little handkerchief I found near Petersburg. I have nothing to send my dear little Robby. But you give him twenty-five cents and tell him pappy sent him it and let him go and buy himself some candy or cakes or something good to eat. Now my dear wife I have not much time to write as our division is on reserve and we have no time to ourselves for we have to move just as the Rebs do. We packed up last night at 12 o'clock and started out at 3 this morning and it was pretty near dinner time when we got back into camp. Again drove in their pickets to their breastworks and about faced and came back. We thought it was the healthiest yet. My dear I begin to think I will soon get home for I have put in the years and now counting the months. I think they will soon slip around. I believe that God will see me safe through if we put our trust in him for he has brought me through many dangers in the last two years and I still have faith in him that he will keep me safe the remainder of my time. Excuse me for not writing more. Write as soon as this comes to hand and tell me all the news. Pay Mr. Plummer if you have the money to spare anyway at all. Give my best respects to him and tell him I am well. I give my love to all inquiring friends and to Mr. Leighty in particular. My love to you my dear wife and my little children. I expect I will get a letter from Jennie when she got that letter and handkerchief. No more at present, may the blessing of God rest with us now and forever. Your affectionate husband,

John W. Brendel

Written to:
Mrs. Ann M. Brendel
Pleasant Unity, Westmoreland Co. Penna.
* Soldiers Letter - Due 3 Cents

> Camp 11th Regt. Weldon Railroad
> 6 miles south Petersburg, Va.
> Sept. the 8th, 1864

Dear Wife:

I sit down to drop you a few lines to let you know that I received two letters since I wrote to you. One dated the 19th and the other the 29th of August and I was very glad to hear from you and feel very thankful to God for his loving kindness towards us all in sparing our unprofitable lives up to the present time. I think if we will put our trust in him he will spare us to meet once more on earth for he has promised in his holy word that what so ever we ask in faith we shall receive. I would have wrote sooner but I was looking every day for a letter from you for you said you would write to me that same week I wrote a letter to my dear little Jennie and sent her a little handkerchief so she could think of me and the hard fighting we had around Petersburg. We are laying six miles south of Petersburg along the Weldon Railroad. We have destroyed the road as far as our line runs along the road. We have been busy building forts and breastworks ever since we came here. We are well fortified here and all along the line. So I think if the enemy attacks us we will make short work of it. I will give you no war news you can see the newspapers and they will tell you better than I can write. The Rebs have a heavy force massed in front of our Corps. It is the 5th Corps. The first and the fifth Corps was consolidated last spring. General Warren is our Corps commander and General Crawford our division and General Banter our brigade. I belong to the 5th Corps, 3rd division, and 2nd brigade. My dear Annie I am not very well today. Trust in God and hope these few scribbled lines may find you enjoying good health and the blessing of God. Now my dear wife I have no more years to serve. I only have months and think if we put our trust in God they will soon pass away. I think I must stop for the present. The sooner you answer this the sooner you will hear from me. Give my love to inquiring friends. No more my love to you and my dear little children. May the blessing of God rest with us all now and forever. Your true and affectionate husband,

J. W. Brendel

Tell Jennie I look to hear from her soon.

Written to:
Mrs. Ann M. Brendel
Pleasant Unity, Westmoreland Co. Penna.
*Soldiers Letter- Due 3 Cents

> Camp 11th Regt. PV.
> near Petersburg Va.
> September 18th, 1864

Dear Wife:

I received your letter this Sunday morning and was glad to hear that you was all well but thought you had forgotten me. I have received no letter from you since the 30th of August and that seems a good while. I had wrote to Jeny and sent her what I thought was a nice handkerchief and a nice paper and you a nice letter and you have not said a word about any of them. So I have nothing to say much till I get a warm letter from you. My dear wife I feel pretty good this Lord's morning and you can't tell how thankful I feel to him for his goodness to me for I have no other being but him to thank. My dear wife I hope these few lines may find you enjoying the same blessing. May God protect us in life and in death. My dear wife my love to you and my dear little children. May God bless you all and I be spared to see you once more. Your affectionate husband,

John W. Brendel

Written to:
Mrs. Ann M. Brendel
Westnewton, Westmoreland Co. Penna.

Fort Dushane 6 miles south of Petersburg Va.
Sept. 26th, 1864

My Dear Wife:

Yours of the 19th came to hand and I was very happy to hear from you once more for I thought you had forgotten me. It had been so long since I got a letter. I had not got a letter from you since the 30th of August and you know that would seem a good while to not hear from the one you loved so much. You know I love you. I do not tell you this to flatter you for you know it yourself. I am enjoying good health at present and Gods will you may be enjoying the same blessing. We have a good fort built here and good breastworks and I expect we will stay here awhile. My dear Anna enclosed you will find ten dollars and if you be a good woman and write to me soon I will send you some more. We will soon have a strong army. The recruits are coming by the thousands nearly every day. Tell Jennie I received some nice documents from my dear little pets and was very glad to think they thought enough of me to send them. I will write to them when I got a little more time and tell them all about everything. There is noting particular going on so I will stop until I get a letter from you. My dear wife and children may God bless and protect you all through life and in death, save you all. Your affectionate husband,

John W. Brendel

There is no express from here. The express office is at City Point and that is about seventeen miles. I have no chance of sending money by express, so I will send it the best I can.

Fort Dushane was located next to the Weldon Railroad south of Petersburg. Currently the Halifax Road runs in the old Weldon Railroad roadbed.[19]

Written to:
Miss Jennie Brendel
Westnewton, Westmoreland Co. Penna.

> Fort Dushane
> 6 miles south of Petersburg Va.
> Sept.27, 1864

Dear Daughter:

I sit down with pleasure to answer your kind and welcomed letter of the 24th. It gave me great pleasure to hear that you was all well and enjoying yourselves. But my dear child you must not forget the great giver of all these great pleasures we enjoy for without him we would be miserable beings. Jenne I am well and enjoying myself as well as can be expected under present circumstances, though if I was at home with you I could enjoy myself a great deal better. Tell Muse that I wrote her a letter yesterday and put ten dollars in it for her and if she answers it pretty soon tell her I will send her some more money. Enclosed you will find one dollar for you and Robbie for spending. For I think you can't enjoy yourselves well without a little bit of change to spend. I sent you a handkerchief and never heard whether you got it or not. I thought it would be such a nice little keepsake. I think I must stop for the present as I have not much time to write. We have drill twice a day and dress parade and roll call and that consumes nearly all the time. My love to you my dear daughter. Give my love to all your little school- mates and to Muss and Robby in particular. I could write ten times as much if I had the time. May God protect you through life and make you a fee and happy child. Love and obey your kind mother and remember your poor old papa at the throne of grace. Your affectionate papa,

J.W. Brendel

I got the nice papers you sent me and was much pleased with them. I am not through reading them yet. I will write to Nanny and Sammy as soon as I can. Don't forget to write.

Written to:
Mrs. Ann M. Brendel
Westnewton, Westmoreland Co. Penna.

           Fort Dushane, Va.
            Oct. 2nd, 1864

Dear Wife:

I received yours of the 26 Sept. and was glad to hear that you was all well. Another battle has commenced on our line. The Corps has all advanced but our brigade and they hold two forts. This one that I am writing in and I don't know what they call the other one. This is Fort Dushane, we have four regiments in this fort and six pieces of artillery and I think we can hold it in spite of all the Rebs can do. Our Corps drove them four or five miles and took three lines of their breastworks and several pieces of artillery and some prisoners. My opinion is that we will whip them so bad this time that they won't show fight anymore. I want you to give Mr. Leighty the money to pay my pole tax and take a receipt for it and send it to me immediately. For I want to give little George B McClellan a hist ? [sic] this time for I think he his the very man to rule our government. We have had enough of the old rail- splitter. Attend to this right on site or you and me won't be good friends. Give my love to all inquiring. My love to you and the children. Your affectionate husband,

J.W. Brendel

I sent you ten dollars and Jennie and Robby one and enclosed you will find five more and if you don't be so slow in writing I will send you some more. I have had only three letters from you since the 30th of August and I don't think that is very punctual writing. I had a notion to commence writing to someone else for I thought you had most forgotten me. You can tear this off and show the other to Leighty.

No more your loving husband,

Jno. W. Brendel

At the Illinois Republican state convention, held on May 9-10, 1860, supporters of Lincoln felt the slogans "Honest Abe" and "Old Abe" seemed colorless. Moved by these opinions, Richard J. Oglesby, a young Decatur politician, located a rail fence which Lincoln and his cousin John Hanks had constructed in 1830. At the convention, two of the rails were brought in decorated with streamers and banners labeled:

Abraham Lincoln
The Rail Candidate
FOR PRESIDENT IN 1860

The rails came from a lot that included nearly 3,000 made in 1830 by Thos. Hanks (actually John) and Abe Lincoln. Abe Lincoln's father was noted as being the first pioneer of Macon County. Of interesting note - he actually was not the first pioneer.

Lincoln confirmed that he built a cabin and split rails thirty years earlier near Decatur.[20]

Written to:
no envelope

Fort Dushane, VA
October 16, 1864

Dear Wife,

I received your two last kind letters and was very glad to hear that you was all well. I am not very well but feel very thankful to the great giver of all the blessings that we enjoy that I am as well as I am. I can't send you any more money this month but I hope I can send you some next month if God spares my life and health and I trust in him for that. You wanted to know if you might buy a piece of carpet. My dear wife, you can just buy what you please. I am satisfied for you know what you need better than I do. I got my tax receipt in time and was one of the judges of the election. Our company went Democratic 14 to 1

Republican. The regiment gave the Republicans a small majority but that was on account so many new men. The army is all laying in camp, quiet. All with the exceptions of a continued picket firing. They kill one occasionally. The army looks first rate and in good health and spirit. The weather is fine two or three frosty nights very pleasant today this is Sunday all very quiet. I have nothing of importance to write. My love to you my dear wife and to Jenny and Robby. May God bless you all and protect you through life and in death and save us all is my sincere prayer. Give my best to all inquiring friends and in particular to Mr. Leighty and G. Plummer. We have three more new forts put up since I last wrote to you. Write soon my dear wife no more but remain your loving husband. Will is well.

John W. Brendel

(To his dear Ann M., the names are close but we are about 800 miles apart by water and railroad. That seems a good distance but I hope it will not be long.)

Now my dear child I have footed that more than twice over since I first started to soldier that's a good distance to walk. I'll tell you all about it when I come home and we will have a many a good joke. Excuse my scribbling.

In October, two days after several state elections had taken place (including Pennsylvania), President Lincoln felt the presidential election was too close for comfort. His opinion was that McClellan would carry Pennsylvania, New York, New Jersey and Delaware.

As days passed Lincoln became more optimistic. Republican strength in Indiana and Ohio turned out to be better than expected. Maryland adopted a constitution outlawing slavery. The soldiers vote was overwhelming Republican. Lincoln encouraged voting in the field and furloughs were granted where possible so soldiers could go home to vote.[21] In the end, Lincoln won the November election with an overwhelming vote of 55% to McClellan's 45%. Lincoln won the electoral vote 221 to 21. He also carried the State of Pennsylvania.[22]

Written to:
Mrs. Ann M. Brendel
West Newton, Westmorland County, Penna.

Fort Dushane, VA
October 19, 1864

Dear Wife,

I received your kind and welcomed letter this morning and was very glad to hear that you was all well. You must not expect a very long letter from me this time for I am not very well. I have a pain in my head and back and feeling under my arm and so you can think I don't feel much like writing. But my dear wife, we must not complain for the good book tells us that all things work to the greater for good. I feel very thankful to God that I am as well as I am and hope to God that these few lines may find you all enjoying good health. I got your two last letters you wrote and answered them. This one you forgot to date it. I received a letter this morning from my sister Elizabeth and she wants you to write to her. I will give you her address and you can write to her. Mrs. Elizabeth Twitchell Greenfield, Green County Illinois. I think I will quit writing for my arm hurts me. Write as soon as this comes to hand. I found some copies I will send them to my dear little Jenny so she can learn to write when I am not there. My love to you my dear wife and children, may God protect you. Your loving husband,

John W. Brendel

To his dear wife, Ann M. Brendel

This is some writing I found and I thought it would make such nice copies for Jenny.

Written to:
Mrs. Ann M. Brendel
West Newton, Westmorland County, Penna.

Fort Wadsworth, VA
October 24, 1864

Dear Wife,

I received your kind and welcomed letter of the 19th and was very happy to hear that you was all well though I am not very well myself. I have a touch of the diarrhea. My arm is pretty near well and I feel very thankful to God for my health being as good as it is and hope these few lines may find you enjoying good health. For I always feel a great deal better when I hear you are all well. I received your two letters that you forgot to date and answered them. If you have a chance to get your winter coal you had better get it for next month is pay month. If kind providence spares my life and health which I hope he will, I will send you twenty or thirty dollars and I supposed Mr. R, Penny can wait for you that long. I almost forgot to tell you this fort is only about a half mile West of Fort Dushane. Our division built both of them and I tell you they are crowders [sic]. I don't think the Johnnies will run against them for it would be of no use. I told you in my last letter that I had got a letter from sister Elizabeth Twichell and she wants you to write to her. She says Mr. Twichell wrote to brother Jacob sometime ago and he never answered it and she would like you to put him in mind of it. You wrote to me sometime ago that Bent Hoke was dead, he is still living yet and as big a devil as ever. Andy Neff was here to see me a couple of weeks ago and looks first rate. Will is well, the weather is dry the air a little cool but pleasant. Tell Jenny that I would like if she would give me a few lines pretty soon and if she learns to write and take care of a good pen. I will try and send her one. I have a gold pen and silver holder worth five dollars and I will send it to her the first chance I get and I think that would be enough her to entice one to learn and I will try and scare up something pretty nice for my dear Robby too. For I think a heap of him and Sammy too. I did send Sammy a dollar when I was at home. I think I will stop for I expect to have more scribbled here than you can read. Write to me soon and often for there is nothing that gives me so much pleasure as to hear from you. Give my love to all enquiring friends, my love to you my dear Anna. May God spare us to meet. Your affectionate husband,

John W. Brendel

On October 27 & 28, Maj. General Hancock led three Union Corps (Second, Fifth and Ninth) from the Petersburg line west towards Boydton Plank Road and the South Side Railroad. Initially, the Union took control of the Boydton Plank Road. However, a Confederate counter attack on the afternoon of the 27th forced the Second Corps to retreat. The Confederates maintained the Boydton Plank Road for the rest of the winter.[23]

Written to:
Mrs. Ann M. Brendel
Westnewton, Westmoreland Co. Penna.

Fort Wadsworth, Va.
Oct. 30, 1864

Dear Wife:

I received you very kind and welcomed letter today while on picket and was very glad to hear from you but was very sorry to hear of you not being well. But hope and pray to God you will be better before these few lines may reach you. I am well and just came off picket. I have been out forty-eight hours. Your brother William was along with me and is well. He was promoted to second lieutenant. The Johnnies are very friendly here in front of us. One of the boys from our post was out yesterday and today and traded newspapers with them. I bought two plugs of tobacco from them for fifty cents per plug in greenbacks. The two plugs was worth two dollars with us. They had plenty of greenbacks and wanted to buy hats, boots, shoes or clothing of any kind and pay us in tobacco or greenbacks. They have plenty of tobacco. The Rebs appear down hearted. They have not much to say in their paper. Our Corps with the Second and Ninth Corps had another fight with them on the 27th and 28th and took a great many prisoners. They claim a victory but we had the best of the bargain. We had a much better position and don't know how much good it did for Butler. He was fighting them on the right and I have not heard what he has done. He is in the rear of Richmond. From here are line is almost around them. Butler had them, drove into their inner entrenchments long ago and is in shelling distance of and could burn it down if it was not for the prisoners and the women and children. Our brigade was not in the fight but was on picket and guarding these forts and indeed I was not very sorry for I tell you I have had as much fight as I want if it can be helped. I would be very glad if it would be settled without another shot if it could be done on fair terms and my sincere prayer is to God that it may soon come to an end and on fair terms and honorable before God and man. Now my dear Annie I think I must bid you goodnight. The drums are beating for roll call and I have had no sleep for two nights. My dear wife I almost forgot to tell you I am well and I hope to God these few lines may find you and family in good health. Write as soon as this comes to hand. I wrote you a letter about the same time you wrote and I expect you got it about the same time I received yours. You must excuse me for not writing more but I am tired and sleepy and I think that a good excuse. Give my love to all inquiring friends. Give my respects to Mr. Leighty and tell him I am very much obliged to him for my tax receipts. I got two I can surly vote now. No more dear Annie. May God keep and protect us. Your affectionate husband,

John W. Brendel

This is Sunday I almost forgot it. Sunday and every day is pretty near alike only we have no drill on Sunday.

(Poem written on the back)

In every joy that crowns my days,

In every pain I bear,
My heart shall find delight and praise,
Or seek relief in prayer

In the previous letter, Brendel was referring to Maj. General Benjamin Butler. Butler was a lawyer from Massachusetts before the war. By October of 1864, Butler was the commander of the Army of the James. General Grant intended to use Butler's two Corps at Petersburg. However, Butler's entire force was bottled up by an inferior Confederate force at Bermuda Hundred, led by General P. T. Beauregard. Butler was ordered home by Grant to await orders. Butler resigned on November 30.[24]

Written to:
Mrs. Annie M. Brendel
Westnewton, Westmoreland Co. Penna.

Camp 11th Regt. PV.
Fort Wadsworth Va.
Nov. the 1st, 64

Dear Wife:

Yours of the 27th came to hand this morning and was duly received and read with great pleasure and was very happy to hear from you and to hear that you was all well now. My dear wife I am in pretty good health and feel very thankful to God for his goodness towards us in sparing our unprofitable lives up to the present moment and hope he will still continue his goodness towards us and permit us to meet once more on earth. That we may see each other face-to-face and that our joys may be full now. Annie my dear you know that all I write to you is love or I would not write. For you know I don't write much to any person. I don't love so you can take it for granted. I love you with my whole heart and if I was to get at and write you a lot of non-

sense you might think I was wanting to flatter you. I never was much of a hand for writing love letters. Now my dear loved Annie I wrote you a long letter on Sunday night after I came off picket and if I had not loved you, you know I would not have stayed up to write you after not sleeping for forty-eight hours. Now my dear love I must tell you how lucky we were the night we came in. The Rebs made a dash and captured a good many of our pickets out of the 2nd division. They killed and wounded several of our pickets. Now my dear child I think I told you pretty near all the particulars in my last letter, so you will have to excuse me for not writing more to you. You asked me if I had wrote to Nancy and Sammy. I did and wish you would see the letter for I think I wrote them a nice one. I did not send them anything yet but I will send them some nice books and papers as soon as I can if God spares my life and health, which I hope he will. Now my dear child you can see that I still live in hope. You must excuse me for calling you a child for you are no child. You are my beloved wife. Your brother William is well he was promoted to 2nd Lieutenant. I think I told you in my last letter. God permit us to meet soon. So we need not write goodnight, my love to you my dear little children. How I wish I was with you this night. How happy I think we would be but Gods will be done, not ours and if we put our trust in him I know that we shall soon meet. Kiss the children for me and give them a father love. May God bless us and make us a happy family. No more but remain your true and loving husband till death,

John W. Brendel

Write soon and tell me just what you think of my letter for I just wrote as it came in to my mind. The drums are beating for roll call, I must go.

Fort Wadsworth was named for General James Wadsworth, a division commander who was killed at the Battle of the Wilderness on May 6, 1864. This fort was built on the grounds of the August 18-19 Battle of

Weldon Railroad. It was constructed to strengthen the Union lines on the south side of Petersburg.[25]

Written to:
Mrs. Ann M. Brendel
West Newton, Westmorland County, Penna.

> Camp 11th Regt. PV near Fort Wadsworth
> November 15, 1864

Dear Wife,

After my love to you I received your two kind and welcomed letters of the first and 8th of November and would have answered them sooner but had not time. We have to drill twice a day and dress parade at sunset and roll call twice a day and that consumes pretty near all the day. I had no candles or I would write at night. We can buy candles from the sutler at fifteen cents per piece. I bought two tonight to write to you for I know I would not get time tomorrow monthly inspection comes off and that takes a good part of the day. My dear Annie, I almost forgot to tell you I am well and in good spirits but feel very thankful to the kind giver of all we enjoy. I was very sorry to hear that you was not well but pray to God that these few scribbled lines may find you enjoying good health. Tell Jenny I was very proud to hear from her and was much pleased with her nice letter she wrote to me. Tell her I am so sorry to tell her I lost that nice gold pen I had for her. Tell her to not be disheartened I will send her something nice yet. I am her pappy and love her if I did lose the pen I was as sorry as she will be I suppose. All is pretty quiet along the line today a little picket firing occasionally. There is nothing strange going on so I think I shall stop for tonight. We have not been paid off yet but look every day for the paymaster. I will send you some money as soon as I am paid. The weather is cool and dry. I sent you that love letter you wanted but you have not answered it yet. Write soon, good night my love to you and the children, kiss them for me. I will write soon your true and faithful husband,

John W. Brendel

Here is a piece of poetry on love I thought I would send it to you as you wanted something on love. I think it very nice you tell me what you think:

ARE OTHER EYES BEGUIILING

Are other eyes beguiling, love?
re other rose-lips smiling, love?
Ah! heed them not, you will not find
Lips more true. Or eyes more kind,
Than mine, love.

Are other white arms wreathing, love?
Are other fond sighs breathing, love?
Ah! heed thew not, but call to mind
The arms, the sighs, you leave behind-
All thine, love.

Gaze not on other eyes, love;
Breathe not for others' sighs, love;
Though you may find a brighter one
Than your own rose, yet there are none
So true, love.

Written by - Ida M. Morford.

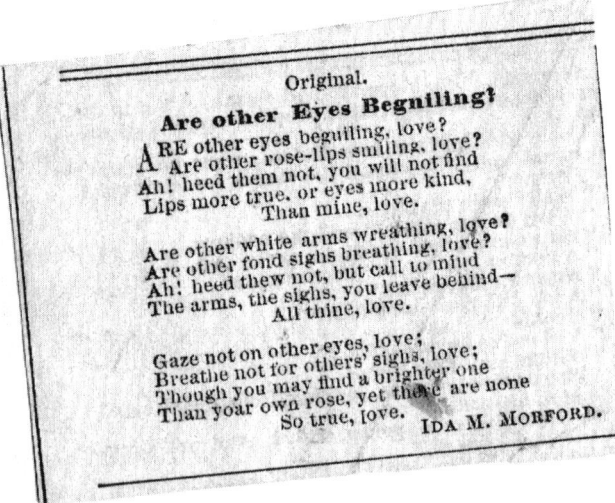

Written to:
Mrs. Anne M. Brendel
West Newton, Westmorland County, Penna.

> Camp 11th Regt. near Fort Wadsworth VA
> November 18, 1864

Dear Wife,

I received your kind and welcomed letters of the 14th and was very glad to hear from you for nothing gives me so much pleasure as to hear from you. But it makes me feel very sorry to hear that you are not well but hope God will restore your health again by the time these few lines may reach you. My health is better now than it has been for two years and I feel very thankful to God the giver of all we enjoy. Now my dear wife, I expect you need some money but I can't send you any just now for we have not been paid yet. But I will send you some as soon as we are paid and I expect that will be before long. I have not much of importance to write as I wrote to you a few days ago. So you will have to excuse this short scribbled letter. I got a letter from Jenny yesterday they are all well Sammy is going to school learns fast, but Jenny says he don't like to go to school and she says she thinks they will have to use some hickory oil if he don't do better. William is well and has his commission and is in command of his company. He makes a first rate looking officer. Our captain is with us now, he only got back a week or so ago. He has been recruiting ever since we was at home. All the rest of the Corps has gone in to winter quarters but our brigade we have very comfortable quarters. I think we will move camp in a day or two and build log houses. They are much warmer then the tents are. The weather is very pleasant. I have only had my overcoat on once or twice this fall but I think this kind of weather wont last long. It's dripping rain now I think we will have a wet spell. Everything is tolerably quiet along the line with the exception of a little cannonading but we have got used to that. I suppose if you was here you would think it pretty rough but we just laugh at it. There is still a few Johnnies comes into our lines every day. They say the women and children are nearly starving at Richmond. They are very thinly plaid that comes in but say they are preparing for four years more war. But I don't think they can stand it that long. I think next summer will wind it up. Anna, I would not care if it was wound up now for I am sick and tired of war. I would like to be at home with my dear wife and little children. Then I think I could enjoy myself for you know there is no peace in time of war. This the 19th I did not get time to finish yesterday. So I will come to a close. It is raining today and is a little colder then it was yesterday. I am on guard today and have not much time to write. My love to you my dear wife and children. Give my respects to all inquiring friends. Your affectionate husband,

Corporal John W. Brendel

Write soon my dear Annie.

Written to:
Mrs. Ann M. Brendel
Westnewton, Westmoreland Co. Penna.

Camp 11th Regt. PV. Fort Wadsworth Va.
Nov. the 21st, 1864

Dear Wife;

I received your kind and welcomed letter dated the 17th last night about 10 o'clock and was very glad to hear from you but was sorry to hear that you was not well. But trust in God that you may be restored to your health again. I am well and feel very thankful for that great blessing. Your brother Will is well and the health of the army is good in general, it has sat in wet. It has been raining ever since I wrote you the last letter. You complain about me not answering your letters. I think I answer all the letters I get from you as soon as I can. Sometimes I get a letter from you when I am on duty and can't answer it just right away but as soon as I can. For instance, I get a letter when on picket. It is three days before I get off. I have not the same opportunity to write as you have I have to write whenever I get the chance and you at home can write whenever you please. So I think you should not complain for my dear wife you know I love you with my whole heart and if it was not for you I would not write much. I have sometimes been thinking about applying for a furlough and come home this winter and I don't know whether to or not. I only have eight months to stay yet till my three years is up and it costs a good bit to get home and back again. It cost me ninety dollars last winter to get home and back. My dear wife we have not been paid yet but as soon as we are I will send you some money. For I expect you stand in need of it. But you will have to shift the best you can till I get paid before long. They should have paid us ten days ago. Everything appears quiet along the line. There is some Johnny comes into our lines every day. I wish they all would come in and then we would not have them to fight and the war would soon be over and then I could come home to my dearest Anny and be a free and happy man once more. How I long to see that day what a happy day that would be. May God spare our lives to see that day soon and we be permitted to meet once more on earth. To part no more while life lasts. No more my dearest dear, my love to you and my dear little children. Kiss them for me and take one for yourself. Write soon your true and faithful husband,

John W. Brendel

Written to:
Mrs. Ann M. Brendel
Westnewton, Westmoreland Co. Va.

Camp 11th Regt. PV. Fort Wadsworth, Va.
Nov. 23, 64

Dear Wife:

I received your kind and welcomed letter last night about 10 o'clock and was very sorry to hear that you was not well but trust in God that you may be better in a few days. My dear it *makes me feel bad to think that you are not well and me so far away from home and no one there to take care of you and my little children. If you think it would be necessary for me to come and by showing the letter I can get a furlough for about twenty or thirty days. Furloughs is only granted for ten days for soldiers to go home on visits. Anny I almost forgot to tell you how my health is. It is good and I thank the good being for it for there is none but him to thank. Anny you complain that I don't answer your letters. Now my dear I think I answer every letter you write to me. Perhaps not as soon as I get them but as soon as circumstances will permit. You know I have my duty to do and that must be done if the plow should stand. I am sure I wrote you two or three every week for the last month. I have wrote you three in the last week. If you want me to come home you can get the doctor to write and I will try and get home for I would like to see you once more for I think it a long time since I saw you. When I was at home it was no satisfaction to you or me for I was so near dead that all I needed was pushed over. But I feel first rate now Anna. I think I could enjoy myself if I was at home. I was not hardly able to get along all summer through the hard fighting. But still got along by the help of God. I footed it every inch of road here from Culpeper. My dear Annie I have not been paid yet. But will send you some money as soon as I am paid and hope that won't be long. I think soldiers should be paid whenever their pay is due to them. For I think they have a hard way of earning their money. It has rained for three or four days and has been cold for two days, froze water in the tent last night. There is five or six Rebs desert every night and come into our lines. It is only a short space that we picket about a mile if they come in all along the line that fast. I think they will soon have no army to fight us and indeed I would not care if they would all come in for I am just as tired if fighting as they are. The deserters that come in say every thing is scarce and dear they say the women and children are nearly starved at Richmond. They say they don't give there soldiers half enough to eat and I guess they pretty near tell the truth. Now my good wife I think I must bid you goodnight, it is going on 10 o'clock. We have had roll call and the taps for lights. If I was with you I could sit and talk to you all night. The pen and ink is a slow* way of talking. It takes so long to get the answer but we should be very thankful that we can talk through the pen and ink. I wrote sister Lizz Twichell a letter and one to Nancy. Jennie answered Nancy's letter. I have not had time to answer it yet but will as soon as I can. Your brother is well. Write soon I must stop may God protect us through life and in death save us. My love to you and the little ones. Your affectionate husband,

John W. Brendel

Here is a piece of poetry for my little Jennie:

A Child's Prayer

Lord pardon all my sins,
But not for aught that I can do,
But for my Saviour's [sic] sake alone,
Who died for sinful children too.

My father, teach me how to pray,
And fill my heart with love to Thee;
And oh! May Jesus to my soul
A Saviour [sic] sweet and precious be.

May I be of that little flock
Who hear and know their Shepherd's call;
May he a shepherd be to me,
My righteousness, my All in all.

Oh, make me gentle, meek and mild,
And pure and holy let me grow,
Till meet for glory, where at last,
For Jesus sake, I hope to go.

Written to:
Mrs. Anne M. Brendel
Westnewton, Westmoreland Co. Penna.

(Written on U.S. Christian Commission stationary)
Fort Wadsworth, Va.
November the 27th, 1864

Dear Wife:

I received your kind letter of the 22nd and was glad to hear from you but was sorry to hear of you being worse but my dear wife I cannot help you. If I was at home I could comfort by kind words. But you will have to trust in God and he will take care of you. I received your letter day before yesterday and could not answer it any sooner. I was relieved today I was on picket. I feel better in health than I have for two years. Get the doctor to write for you stating it is necessary for me to come home and I can get a furlough for twenty or thirty days. They only give ten day furloughs to go home on visits. It would take eight days for me to get home and back and that would not be worthwhile hardly to go home for such a short time. My dear I don't feel like writing. If I was with you I could sit and talk to you all night for I have not slept any for two nights. There is nothing strange going on here. You will have to excuse me for not writing more to you. May God restore your health and take care of you until we meet and I hope that will be soon. Write to me as soon as this comes to hand for you know I will have no rest till I hear from you. If you are not able to write get someone to write for you. My dear I have not been paid yet but as soon as we are I will send you money. I have a good leaver Wach? (ed. leather watch). I would sell it but I can hardly do without it on account of putting on reliefs [sic] when on picket. If I thought you was in want of anything I would sell it. If you are let me know and I will sell it and send you the money. My love to you my dear hoping these few lines may find you better. Give my love to my dear little children and kiss them for me. No more, write soon. Your affectionate husband,

John W. Brendel

Written to:
Mrs. Ann M. Brendel
Westnewton, Westmoreland Co. Penna.

> Camp 11th Regt. PV.
> Fort Wadsworth Va.
> Nov. 29th, 64

My Dear Wife:

I received your kind and welcomed letter this evening and feel very thankful to God that we are still spared to write to one another if we can't talk to each other. I feel sorry to hear that you are no better yet but I hope God will spare our lives to meet once more on earth. If we put our trust in him the blood of Christ "cleans us from all sins, he that believeth shall be saved." It seems then that all the sins of every believer are forgiven. Can any blessing be more complete? So my dear wife if we put our trust in him he will not forsake us in the hour of need. I got the papers the children sent for me and was very proud of them. They went to the 11th cavalry and was sent to me. I sent three papers one for you and one for Jenny and one for Robbie. The one headed, The Phuney Phellow [sic] is for Robert. My dear I will have to quit it is getting late. If you get worse do as I told you in my last two letters and I will try and get home. There is strong talk of our regiment going to Lake Erie. I wish it would for you don't know how tired I am of old Virginia. My dear Annie I don't feel any to well myself tonight. My back pains me considerable. I don't think my back will ever be as sound as it was. There is nothing strange going on here so I think I will quit, write soon. We have not been paid yet. There is still a few Rebs come into our lines everyday. Good night my dear wife. May God bless and protect us all now and forever. Still remain your true and loving husband,

John W. Brendel

Here is a little book for my dear Jenny

Written to:
Mrs. Anna M. Brendel
Westnewton, Westmoreland Co. Penna.

> Fort Wadsworth, Va.
> December 2nd, 64

Dear Wife:

Your kind and welcomed letter of the 28th of Nov. came to hand last night after I was in bed. I got up and lit the candle with great anxiety to hear from you but was sorry to hear that you was no better yet. But feel thankful to God for his goodness toward us in sparing our lives to the present time while thousands younger than we are called off and we are still spared. Oh how thankful we should be to God for his goodness towards us and restore us both to health again on earth that our joys may be full. I have been doctoring for my back the last two days. We had a review today or I would wrote this morning. You would got it a day sooner. There is nothing strange going on here only some Reb prisoners coming in to our lines every day. There was two out of our regiment deserted last night and went over to the Rebs. Our pickets fired at them but did not hit them. They were both out of Company D, both Welsh men. Our cavalry made a raid on the South Side Railroad and tore up ten miles of it and captured one hundred-ninety prisoners, five pieces of artillery, burned one locomotive and train of cars and destroyed a great amount of government stores for them. We have not been paid yet. I will send you money as soon as we get paid. I think I will have to stop as I have no news of importance to write to you, my love to you my dear. Kiss my little pets for me and give them a fathers love. Your brother Will is well. No more write soon. May God spare us to meet soon. Your Affectionate husband,

John W. Brendel

I think it has all blown over about us getting back to Pennsylvania. I don't hear anymore talk of it.

Written to:
Mrs. Jennie Brendel
Westnewton, Westmoreland Co. Penna.
(In care of Mrs. Ann M. Brendel)

                                             Fort Wadsworth, Va.
                                               December 4th, 64

Dear Daughter:

It is with pleasure that I sit down to write to you to answer your request, but if you want to keep up correspondence you must answer all the letters I wrote to you. I wrote last and you did not answer it but your mother said you wanted me to write and I thought I would as this is Sunday and me being excused from duty on account of my back. I have been doctoring for three days and it is a little better. I have a blister on now and that makes it pain me more than it would. My sincere prayer is that these few lines may find you in good health. I feel uneasy about your kind mother being sick. But my dear Jennie my sincere prayer is that God will restore her to health again and we may all meet once more. Jennie you must be a good girl and God will reward you for it. I wrote your mother a letter yesterday and sent you a little book in with the letter and I sent three papers. One for mother and one for you and one for Robie. The Phuney Phellow? [sic] was for Robie. I thought as he could not read he could take a good laugh at the pictures. Good children can take a good laugh for the good book tells us Gods people are a lively people and full of good works. Jennie I must stop it is time for the mail to start. If mother is now better tell her to do all I wrote to her to do and I will try hard to get home. Jennie I think I could enjoy myself if I was at home with you. Now my dear Jennie I could write a heap more to you if I had time. But you must write soon and I will write again to you. Give my love to your poor mother and tell her that pap loves her as he does his own sole. I must stop by giving you and Robie my love. Give my love to all inquiring friends and your little Sunday school mates. Your affectionate father,

John W. Brendel

Written to:
Mrs. Anna M. Brendel
Westnewton, Westmoreland Co. Penna.

(ed. Written on Sanitary Commission Stationary)
City Point Hospital
Dec. 8th, 64

My Dear Wife:

I wrote you a few lines yesterday from division hospital to let you know where I am. I left there last night and got here about 12 o'clock last night. The Corps left and I was not able to go along and I had to go to the hospital. The talk is that they are going to Weldon City, North Carolina if they are successful. I received one letter from you last Sunday and one yesterday morning. I had just put one in the mailbag for my dear little Jennie. My dear I will send you an envelope with my address and I want you to write as soon as you get this for I want to hear from you so bad. I may be moved from here before I get an answer from you for we may be here today and away tomorrow. My dear wife I will try and get a furlough as soon as I am paid. We have nearly four months pay coming. Four months for me will be seventy-two dollars. If you get worse get somebody to write for you if you have no doctor and I will try to get home. These last two days seem the longest days I have put in for sometime. I will have to quit for the mail starts out in a few minutes. I feel well enough only my back and it pains me considerable. I would have gone along with the regiment if I thought I could stood the marching. You had better see Plummer about the house and tell him that we have not been paid for nearly four months and as soon as I am paid you will pay him and I hope that will be before long. May God grant these few lines to find you in good health. Your affectionate husband,

Corporal J. W. Brendel

My love to Jennie and Bobbie and a good share for yourself.

Even though Union forces disrupted the overall use of the Weldon Railroad, Confederates still managed to use it for transporting supplies. On December 7, the Fifth Corps was sent to attempt the complete destruction of the railroad. On December 8, they burned ties, heated and bent rails. The Corps returned to camp near Petersburg on December 12.[26]

Written to:
Mrs. Ann M. Brendel
West Newton, Westmoreland Co. Penna.

(Written on Sanitary Commission Stationary)
City Point Hospital
Saturday, Dec10th, 1864

My Dear Wife:

I just thought as I had nothing to do I might as well write you a few lines to let you know how I am getting along. I feel first rate with the exception of my back and it is no better. But I feel very thankful to god for his goodness to me and hope the God of mercy may grant that these few lines may find you enjoying good health once more. I have nothing of importance to write to you as I have wrote three letters to you since I left for here. The weather is pleasant overhead. It snowed and sleeted last night. The ice is two or three inches thick. It is thawing and is very cloudy. I think it will rain before night. There is news came in today that our Corps has gone to Weldon City. I don't know whether it is true or not but you will see the whole proceedings in the papers before this reaches you. I want you to write soon for I am so anxious to hear from you for when I don't get a letter from you for so long I get so disheartened I hardly know what to do for God knows my only care is for you and my little children. My sincere prayer is that God will take care of you till we meet again. Now write to me soon and direct to City Point Hospital 5th Corps. I wrote you a letter yesterday and dropped it in the Christian Commission box and I want you to let me know whether they put a stamp on it or not. Some of the soldiers say they put stamps on and some say not so, I just want to know.

Here is a nice little book. I read it today and I thought you and Jennie might like to read it too. We have good comfortable beds here and pretty good grub. A little more would not hurt but we have no reason to complain at all. There are some seven or eight hundred sick and wounded here. There is twenty-seven in the tent I am in. They are all able to help themselves and complain they don't get enough to eat. I have enough and I am taking no medicine. As it is nearly mail time I must wind up, my love to you and my sear little pets. Kiss them for me. May God bless us all and permit us to meet soon is my sincere prayer. Your true and most obedient husband,

Corporal John

Direct to:
Corporal John W. Brendel
5th Corps Hospital
City Point, Va.

Written to:
Miss Jenny Brendel
West Newton, Westmoreland Co. Penna.
(In care of Ann M. Brendel)

(Written on Sanitary Commission Stationary)
5th Corps Hospital
City Point, Va.
Sunday Dec. 11th, 1864

My Dear Daughter:

I sit down to drop you a few lines to let you know how I am getting along. Thank God I am pretty well with the exception of my back. My dear daughter I hope these few lines may find you enjoying good health for that is one of the greatest blessings we can have. I wrote you a letter last Sunday if you did not answer it, it went to the regiment and I don't know whether ever I will get it or not. So you had better direct your letters here and try and write soon for I would like to hear from you and my dear little Robert and your poor sick mother. You must cheer her up and tell her pap loves her too and tell her to keep in good spirits. Pap will soon come home and then we will have a happy time if we be good people and love God and do his will. Now Jenie the lost is found, I got the gold pen again and I will send it to you in this letter in a little book. So you can read the book and write with the pen. But Jennie I am sorry to tell you I loaned it to Mr. Steel to write a love letter and it got broke. But you can use it till I get home and then I can get a new holder. The pen cost two dollars and fifty cents without the holder. Now my dear Jennie I have not much of importance to write to you as I have wrote a letter home everyday last week. I guess Muse will get tired of reading so much nonsense. The weather is still wet and cool. The ground is nearly covered with ice. I will close, my love to you all. Give my love to your little schoolmates and tell them I send my love to them all. May God save us all is your father's prayer. Your affectionate father to his daughter,

John W. Brendel

Jennie Write soon

At the time of the previous letter, James Steele was a 1st Sergeant. Steele mustered in on March 18, 1864. He was commissioned a 2nd Lieutenant June 30, 1865 and mustered out with his regiment July 1, 1865.

Written to:
Mrs. Ann M. Brendel
Westnewton, Westmoreland Co. Penna.

Fifth Corps Hospital, City Point, Va.
Monday, Dec.12, 64

Well Annie:

As I had nothing to do I thought I would drop you a few lines to let you know how I am this morning. My back is no better. I am not taking any medicine. If I could only hear from you this morning it would be all the medicine I would want for I feel uneasy about you. But I trust in God to take care of you and me too. I was at church last evening and we had a good meeting. There was about two-hundred soldiers and four ladies. They looked like angels. It put me in mind of home to see them and hear them sing. They were splendid singers and I suppose Christians too. I have wrote you a letter every day since I have been in the hospital but yesterday and I wrote one to Jennie yesterday and sent the gold pen to her. I found it again and loaned it to James Steel to write a letter and got the holder broke and I put it in that old holder so the pen would not get broke and when I get home I will try and get her a nice holder for it. For I think she is a good girl and deserves something nice. That pen cost two dollars and fifty cents in Pittsburg. The holder and pen cost five dollars. I was so sorry it got broke for it had such a nice holder, but is no use to cry for spilt milk. Now Annie you will have to shift the best you can till I get paid. I have seventy-two dollars coming to me the first of January. They should have paid us long ago for I think a soldier has a hard way of earning their money and need it too as they earn it. My dear wife I tell you I am down on the present administration. We never have better times than when we are under a good old democratic administration. We have got to give two or three dollars in paper to get one in gold. I must stop or you will think I am a politician. Politics don't bother me but I would like to have my money whenever I earn it and then I think my family would not want for anything. This is the first time I have ever been away from my regiment yet and I don't feel contented. I would like to see the boys and be with them what time I have to stay in the army. But so it goes I was not able to go along and I suppose this is the best place I can be under present circumstances. I heard today that our Corps destroyed fifteen miles of the South Side Railroad. There has been no wounded come in yet and they have been gone nearly a week. So I think they have had good luck and my sincere prayer is that it will soon be over. That we can return home to our dear wives and live in peace once. My dear Annie if I was with you today how happy I would feel. My paper is all. My love to you and pray that we may meet soon. Your affectionate husband,

Corporal John

To his dear Annie forever.

Written to:
Mrs. Ann M. Brendel
Westnewton, Westmoreland Co. Pa.

(ed. Written on United States Christian Commission Stationary)
City Point Hospital
December the 18th, 1864

Dear Wife:

After my love to you I would inform you that I am detailed here at this hospital. I do not know how long I will stay. I may not stay three days and I may stay my time out. I am not able to do duty in the regiment but I can do as much good here as a stout able bodied man can. I feel very uneasy about you. I wrote you on the 7th when I started to go to the hospital and wrote to you every day since. Only the last three days I was waiting to get a letter from you. You can't tell how disappointed I feel when I go to the office and look over the list of letters and none for poor me. I feel almost forsaken. I traded my watch off for another watch and got fifteen dollars to boot and I wanted to send you some money for you to take your Christmas spree. But I did not know if you was living or not as I have not heard from you for so long. If you are not able to write you might get someone to write for you. I wrote to George Plummer. I suppose he will answer my letter pretty soon he always does. My dear Annie I hope these few scribbled lines may find you and my dear little children in good health for that is the greatest blessing we can ask for. Now my dear Annie I think I will stop. Maybe I will get a letter from you pretty soon and then I will write to you again. If I can get down to the express office I will express ten dollars to you tomorrow and if not I will send it by mail. I would have sent it to you two or three days ago if I had got any word from you. Maybe you don't direct your letters correct. You must direct in this shape-

Corporal John W. Brendel
5th Corp Hospital
City Point, Va.

We have not been paid yet. I think we will have a poor rotten government as long as the Republicans are in power. A man must be kept here from his family and can't even get his money he has earned hard to send to his family. I could say a heap on the subject but I don't think worthwhile. My love to you my dear wife may God bless you and protect you till we meet again is your affectionate husband's prayer. Yours in love,

John W. Brendel

At the heading of the previous letter (in pre-printed type) the purpose of the United States Christian Commission is explained:

> Individual Relief department:
> The United States Christian Commission seeks to afford a sure and effective medium of communication between the wounded or sick soldier-whether in the camp or in the Field or General Hospitals-and his home friends. This is done by furnishing facilities for writing and by writing for those who are not themselves able. Soldiers, for whom inquires are made of us, will be sought out if possible and relieved and their condition made known to those asking. All letters of this character should give the Corps, Division, Regiment, and Company of the

soldier, as also the Hospital in which he is suppose to be. Address United States Christian Commission, 500 H Street, Washington, D.C.

Another agency which provided a valuable service, was the United States Sanitary Commission. Established by the War Department on June 9, 1861, the Commission was organized, funded and operated by civilians. The Commission was divided in three departments: Preventive Services, General Relief and Special relief. Preventive Services sent medical inspectors to visit camps, hospitals and transports. The inspectors checked on dangers from climate change, exposure, malarious causes, hard marching or any failure of supplies or transportation. The Department of General Relief supplied food, clothing, bandages furniture and medicines for wounded soldiers in camp, field, post, regimental or general hospitals. The Special Relief Department provided the Soldiers Homes. These homes furnished shelters, food and medical care to men who could not get it from the government or were permanently discharged from hospitals.[27]

Written to:
Miss Jennie Brendel
Westnewton, Westmoreland Co. Penna.
(In care of Mrs. Ann M. Brendel)
*Soldiers Letter

> City Point, Va.
> December the 19th, 1864

Dear Jennie:

I have nothing to write to you till I get a answer from the two letters I wrote to you. Enclose you will find five dollars for mother and you must make her give you your Christmas gift out of it. I think I won't write until I get a letter from some of you. I thought when I wrote to you and Muss everyday I would get plenty of letters but so I get none. My love to you all my dear Jennie, your affectionate father,

John W. Brendel

Written to:
Mrs. Ann M. Brendel
Westnewton, Westmoreland Co. Penna.
*Soldiers Letter

City Point Hospital, Virginia
Dec. 19th, 1864

Dear Wife:

I just thought as you would not write to me I would write to you for spite and enclosed you will find five dollars for a Christmas gift and I know that will make you madder yet and I wrote Jennie and put five dollars in it for you. I thought that it would be the safest way to send it. I traded my watch off and got fifteen dollars to boot and got a nice hunters case watch worth fifteen dollars. It is a little out of repair but I can get it fixed for a couple of dollars. If I was at home I could get it fixed for fifty cents. I have nothing more to write to you as I have been here for nearly two weeks and got no letter from you. I thought as I was here you would be very punctual in writing. I don't think there is any excuse for you unless you are not able to write and if you are not able then you must have got someone to write for you, no more but my love to you and family. Your affectionate husband,

Corporal John W.

Now Annie try and write if you please. I will give you my address one more and I don't think I will write to you any more until I hear from you.

Corporal John W. Brendel
Fifth Corps Hospital
City Point, Va.

N.B. I am detailed here but I don't know how long I may stay and I feel very anxious to hear from you. Your loving, J.W.B

Written to:
Mrs. Ann M. Brendel
Westnewton, Westmoreland Co. Penna.

(ed. Written on United States Sanitary Commission Stationary)

City Point Hospital, Va.
December 23, 64

My Dear Wife:

I just sat down to drop you a few lines to let you know I am going back to my regiment tomorrow. You can direct your letters to the regiment as usual. I have had only one letter from you since I came to the hospital. That was dated Dec. the 16th. I will write as soon as I get to the regiment. No more but remain your affectionate husband,

John W. Brendel

When you get this let me know if you got the money I sent and all the particulars. I did not write to you much as I have wrote you a letter nearly every day since I have been here.

Written to:
No Envelope

Camp 11th Regt. P.V.
Jerusalem Plank Road, Va.
December 26, 1864

Dear Wife:

I sit down to drop you a few lines to let you know I am back with the regiment again and I am as well as can be expected. I dropped you a few lines on Saturday when I left the hospital to let you know where I was. I thought I would write again for fear you might not get the letter I wrote. I am so busy building my house. I have hardly time to write. I sent you your Christmas gift when I was at the hospital and I feel very uneasy to hear *whether you got it or not. I received two letters from you since I came back and such a nice letter from Liza. I will send it to you when I answer it. Your Christmas gift was ten dollars and Robbie thirty cents. But you was to give Jennie hers out of yours. Write as soon as this comes to hand and as soon as I get my house done I will write again. Let me know all the particulars, my love to you and the children. Give my good wishes to all inquiring folks and to Mrs. S. Shaffer and family. No more at present but remain your loving husband,*

John W. Brendel

To his dear Annie M.

By the end of 1864, prospects of the Confederacy winning the war were dim. Lee's ranks were stretched thin while Grant was receiving additional troops. Lee was losing as much as a regiment a day just to desertion alone. General Ewell wrote to Lee stating he had only eight-hundred men to guard a line formally manned by two-thousand.[28]

In the South, Maj. General William Sherman's army captured Savannah, Georgia on December 21. Sherman presented the City of Savannah to President Lincoln as a Christmas gift. Lee could not afford to send troops in support of Savannah.

On the other side, General Grant experienced some concerns of his own. The armies were in the same relative position as six months ago (before Petersburg). Grant was afraid the Confederates may escape by rail southward towards Danville. Grant was impatient to commence a spring campaign, but the roads were impassible for artillery and wagons and he wanted Sheridan's cavalry with him.[29]

December 23 /64

City Point Hospittle Va

My dear wife

I just sot dow to drop you a fiew lines to let you know I am going back to my Reg't to murow you can direct your letters to the Reg't as usial I have had only one letter from you since I came to the Hospittle that was dated Dec the 16th I will write as soon as I get to the Reg't No more but remain Your Afectnate Husband
John W Brendel

when you get this let me know if you got the mony I sent and all the particulars

Letter written on Sanitary Commission stationary.

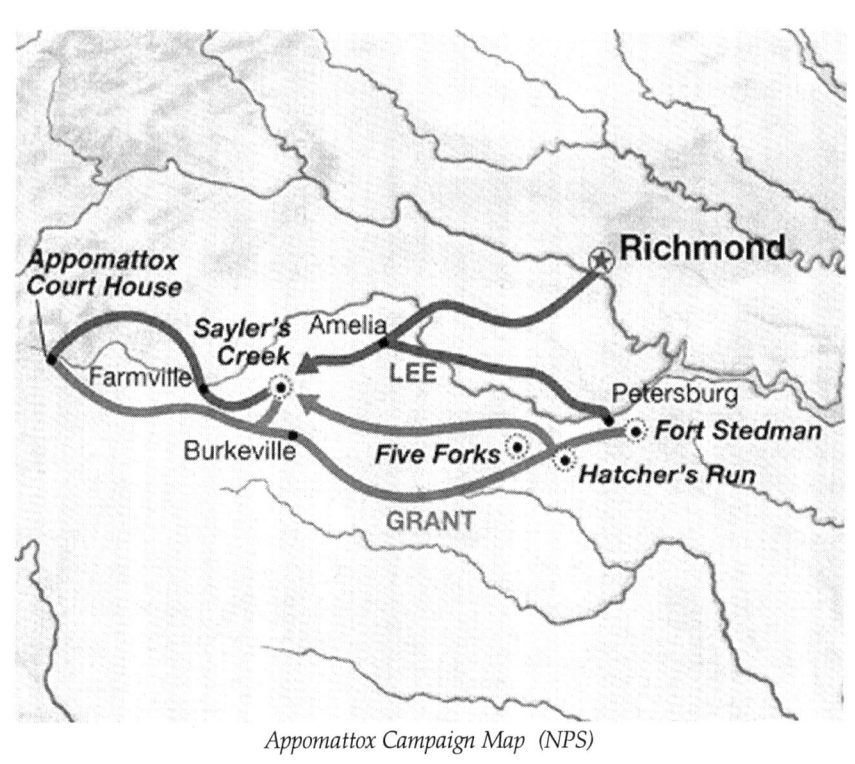

Appomattox Campaign Map (NPS)

Chapter 4

1865-Rebs Are Deserting

Written to:
Mrs. Ann M. Brendel
Westnewton, Westmoreland Co. Penna.
*Soldiers Letter

Camp 11th Regt. P.V.
Jerusalem Plank Road
January 5, 1865

Dear Wife:

I sit down this evening to drop you a few lines to let you know how I am getting along. I am not very well at present but hope these few lines may find you in good health. I received a letter from you and Jennie last Sunday morning and was very glad to hear from you and would have answered it right on sight but I had to go on picket and had not time until this evening and I was waiting on an answer from that money I sent you on the 19th of December. Now this makes fifteen days since I sent it to you and I think it very strange that any time I send any money to you it is so long before I hear from it. Now my dear Annie I will stop for the night as I am not very well. For you know a body can't write a good letter when they don't feel right. So you will have to excuse me this time. Now my dear wife you will please answer this as soon as this comes to hand and it may be possible that we will be paid till I get an answer from this. We was mustered up for two months pay the first of the month again. They keep mustering us for pay whether we are ever paid or not. If you are now better you can write to me stating how you are and how bad you want to see me and I will send the letter to the general asking him for a furlough to go home to see you. Good night my dear wife may God bless you and my dear little pets till I see you again. No more but a husbands love,

John W. Brendel

Written to:
No Envelope

> Camp 11th Regt. P.V.
> Jerusalem Plank Road
> January 10th, 1865

Dear Wife:

I received your two last welcomed letters and was very glad to hear from you and that you was getting better again. The last was dated the 4th. You wanted my advice about the house I want you to use your own judgment about that for you know what would suit you better than I could tell you. They are giving furloughs to soldiers that have sick relations. You might get Tommy Sikes or someone else to write a few lines to me stating your case and how anxious you are to see me and write about yourself. Make your case as bad as possible and I will send it in with the application for a furlough to come home. I think we will be paid by the time you answer this. I want you to tell me in your next how brother Jacob is and how he is getting along. I heard here that he had married very rich. I have nothing of importance to write but hope I will soon get home then I can tell you more than I can write. You wanted to know how your brother Will is, that is more than I can tell you. I suppose he is well. I have only seen him once since I came back. He is promoted to first lieutenant and makes a very good officer. His company lays on the right of the regiment and my company on the extreme left and you know I don't go visiting very much. I was very glad to hear that you got the ten dollars I sent you. I thought you would get it for a Christmas gift. I mailed it on the 19th of December and thought you would get it by the 24th. I received your letters last Sunday and was on Guard and not time to write to you any sooner. Fred Overly came back Sunday evening and brought back the tobacco you sent me and it was very nice. I had just got a pound from the sutler but this you sent is a great deal better. I got the tracts you and Jennie sent me but have not time to read them yet. I am not very well but feel a great deal better than when I last wrote. I will close by giving you my love. If you write as I told you I will try and come home. No more but remain your affectionate husband,

John W. Brendel

(ed. Written on the same paper)

January 11th

I wrote you this last night and was taking it to the office and got a letter from you dated the 5th. I opened this again to let you know that I got the tobacco. Overly is back again to the regiment. It has rained very hard here for the last day and cleared up last night and is very pleasant today. You do as I told you in this letter and I will try to get home on a furlough. No one can get a furlough without some excuse.

I got the letter Jennie wrote. It was sent to the hospital and was sent on.

Written to:
Mrs. Ann M. Brendel
West Newton, Westmorland County, Penna.
*Soldiers Letter- Due 3 Cents

> Camp Third Division, Fifth Army Corps.
> Ambulance Department
> January 14, 1865 Virginia

My Dear Wife,

As I had nothing to do this morning I thought I would drop you a few lines to let you know where I am and how I am getting along. I am well thank God and getting along first rate. I have been promoted to Sergeant and detailed in the ambulance department and have an easy birth of it. I have a good horse to ride and no gun or knapsack to tote along, no picket or skirmishing to do. I have three ambulance teams in charge and see to getting the wounded off the field. Sergeant Hile [sic] not Jim was promoted to lieutenant and I just stepped into his boots and it was a good step for me. Now my dear, Annie as I have no news of importance to write at present. I think I shall close by giving you my address so you can write to the sergeant. This is the way you will have to direct;

Sergeant John W. Brendel
Ambulance Department
Second Brigade, Third Division, Fifth Army Corps.
Washington, DC

No more at present my dear but my love to you and my dear children and God knows I love you, your affectionate husband,

John W. Brendel

Write soon and tell me all the particulars about town.

Early in the Civil War, wounded soldiers were removed from the battlefield in a haphazard fashion. Frequently, the most unfit soldiers were detailed to the duty of caring for the wounded. During the first year, it was not uncommon for the assistants to get drunk off medical liquor, ignore their comrades and hide from enemy fire.[1]

Hand litters were used to evacuate soldiers. The most effective litters weighed twenty-four pounds and had collapsible legs so they could serve as a temporary cot. A soldier's comrades sometimes used make shift stretchers. Poles or muskets passed over coat sleeves or blankets to form a stretcher.[2]

In August 1862, Medical Director Jonathan Letterman convinced General McClellan (who was a good organizer of soldiers) to initiate an Ambulance Corps under the direction of the Medical Department. The ambulances moved together with the division. The following is excerpts from General McClellan's General Order No. 147 dated August 2, 1862:

1. The ambulance Corps will be organized on the basis of a captain to each army corps as the commandant of the ambulance corps, a first lieutenant for a division, second lieutenant for a brigade, and a sergeant for a regiment.

2. The allowance of ambulances and transport carts will be 1 transport cart, 1 four-horse and 2 two-horse ambulances for a regiment; 1 two-horse ambulance for each battery of artillery, and 2 two-horse ambulances for the headquarters of each army corps. Each ambulance will be provided with two stretchers.

3. The privates of the ambulance corps will consist of two men and a driver to each ambulance and one driver to each transport cart.

4. The sergeant in charge of the ambulance corps for a regiment shall conduct the drills, inspection, under the orders of the commander of the brigade ambulance corps.

In addition, during a march no one was allowed to ride on an ambulance without the authority of the medical officers. Any illegitimate baggage was left along the road if no room was available in the baggage wagons. Only good serviceable horses were to be used for the ambulances and were not taken for any other purpose.[3]

During a battle, the medical officers would establish stations (aid) as close to the firing line as possible. Their wounds were dressed and they were set aside or started to walk towards a field hospital. As soon as possible, the ambulance train approached and took over care of the wounded. If the ambulance could not reach the wounded, litters were utilized to carry the wounded back to the ambulance. The ambulance transported the wounded to a field hospital. Field hospitals were located just out of artillery range. If additional treatment and rehabilitation was required, the patient was transported to a general hospital. Patients were transported to general hospitals by train or steamboat when possible. General hospitals were usually located near larger cities.[4]

Written to:
Mrs. Ann M. Brendel
West Newton, Westmorland County, Penna.

Third Division Ambulance Department
January 30, 1865

My Dear Annie,

Your kind and welcomed letters of the 24th and 25th came to hand and was read with great pleasure and how glad I was to hear of you all enjoying good health for that is the greatest blessing we can enjoy and how thankful we should be. I am in first rate health, better than I have been for the last two years and I think I can easy stand it out these few months I have to stay when I stood it so long. My opinion is that the war will be over inside of three months. I don't think the Rebs can stand it much longer. The deserters are coming in everyday all along the line in front of us and say they can't stand it long. My dear Annie, I feel glad that you have rented a house for your mind will be at ease. I have not been paid yet but as soon as I am I will send you the money to pay off your debts and start you on fair footing again and I think by the time you are broke again I will be at home. Davie Burkhart died after that last raid on the Weldon Road, he was a good soldier. I saw Billie Armae [sic] yesterday, he is well and looks first rate. All the West Newton boys are close here. George Brush, [sic] was to see me the other day. I was not at home I saw Fulmer's boys yesterday and Bent Hoke they are all well. Young Fulmer belongs to the same regiment Andy Neff does. Now my dear wife, I think as I have nothing of importance to write to you I shall come to a close by giving you my love till I come home write soon. You wanted to know what capital A.C. stood for, it stands for army corps. No more at present but remain your true loving sergeant,

John W. Brendel

Davie Burkhart enlisted in the 155th Pennsylvania Infantry on August 22, 1862. Burkhart died at City Point, Virginia on January 6, 1865.

Written to:
No Envelope

Ambulance Department
February 4, 1865

My Dear Wife,

I sit myself down to answer your kind and welcomed letter of the 31st that came to hand today and was duly read with great pleasure to hear that you was all well. I feel thankful to kind province for his goodness in sparing our lives and health. I thought as we are under marching orders I would drop you a few lines to let you know that I am well. I saw Brother William day before yesterday. He is well and in good spirits now. My dear Annie, I don't want you to make yourself uneasy about me for God is able to take care of you and me too if we put our trust in him. Now my dear child you will have to shift along the best you can till I am paid. I don't think we will be paid off till the first of next month as there is no sign of the pay master yet. There is six months pay coming to me. I think that's too long between pay days for poor soldiers whose families have to depend on their wages to keep them. I got a letter from Jenny today they are all well and Sammie was making a sled while Jenny was writing to me. Write as soon as this comes to hand for it makes me feel cheerful to hear from home. There is nothing of importance going on at present only a little ball playing in front of Petersburg. I suppose if you was here you would think it pretty rough play. It has been very quiet along the lines for the last few days. The weather has been cold for the last month. It is warm and pleasant here today, we had once this winter a snow about two inches deep. I have only had my overcoat two or three times this winter. It is not half so cold here as it is in Pennsylvania. Now Annie, I think I will stop for this time by giving my love to you and my dear little pets. Kiss them for me and tell them to be good children till I come. Direct as usual to the Ambulance Department. No more but remain your affectionate husband,

John W. Brendel

N.B. Here is a letter from sister Lizza and her husband. I thought maybe you would like to read it and write to them.

Written to:
Mrs. Ann M. Brendel
Westnewton, Westmoreland Co. Penna.
*Soldiers Letter - Due 3 Cents

Ambulance Department
Feb. 11th, 1865

My Dear Annie:

I have just got back to camp and thought I would drop you a few lines to let you know that I am still living and well. We have had a pretty hard trip of it this time. We have just been gone one week. We started last Sunday morning and this is Saturday night. I dropped you a few lines last Sunday morning. I don't know whether you got them or not and sent you Lizzies letter. We started on Sunday morning at 6 o'clock and marched till night and then encamped till morning started and went about two miles and commenced fighting and fought till Tuesday night till about 12 o'clock. Lost over one hundred killed, wounded and missing in our regiment. Lieutenant William McLaughlin and myself are two of the lucky ones that came out without being hurt. It has been cold, raining and freezing nearly every day since we have been gone. Now my dear wife I will stop as I feel very tired and sleepy. You may judge I don't feel much like writing but maybe you can make out how to read it. I got one letter from you while on the raid dated Feb.2nd and was so glad to hear from you. Write as soon as you get this for I am so anxious to hear from you. No more may God permit us to meet soon. My love to you and my dear little children. Your affectionate husband,

John W. Brendel

Even during the winter, Grant wanted to keep pressure on Lee. On February 5, Grant sent the Second and Fifth Corps to take Boydton Plank Road at Hatchers Run. The Confederates battle line was now extended to thirty-seven miles.[5] On the morning of the 7th, the 11th Pennsylvania (in support of the 39th Massachusetts) engaged with the enemy. Through several skirmishes, the enemy was pushed back. A temporary earthwork was captured and forces advanced within one-hundred yards of a strong fortification. They camped for the night on the field. The following day they were placed again on the skirmish line. On the 10th, the 11th Pennsylvania returned to camp having lost nine killed, sixty-nine wounded and nine missing.[6]

Written to:
Mrs. Ann M. Brendel
Wesrtnewton, Westmoreland Co. Penna.

Ambulance Department, Va.
Feb. 16th, 1865

Dear Wife:

I sit down this evening to answer your kind and welcomed letter of the 6th that came to hand today and was glad to hear that you were all living but sorry to hear that you was not well. But trust in God that you will be well before this reaches you. I am as well as usual and feel very thankful to the good being for his goodness towards me in sparing my life and health through the last hard raid. We had two days hard fighting and lost a good many good men and officers too. We started Sunday morning the 5th and got back on Saturday. We marched all day on Sunday and fought Monday and Tuesday till about 12o'clock Tuesday night. It was very cold and freezing Tuesday it rained and sleeted all day and you can judge what kind of time we had. But I did not mind it much myself but it was hard on the poor wounded soldiers. Now my dear wife I have nothing of importance to write to you as I wrote you a letter on Sunday morning before I started on the raid and one on Saturday just as soon as I got back and got my supper and horse fed and have got no answer from either of them but hope I may tonight when the mail comes in. I have not seen brother William since Sunday. I visited the brigade last Sunday and it will be my turn tomorrow again. We have not been paid of yet but I hope soon. Just as soon as I am paid I will send you some money for I expect you need it bad enough. For I need some myself. I have no postage stamps. Now my dear Annie I think I will stop and tell you all about things in general when I come home. The Johnny Rebs still keep deserting. There was sixty come into our lines last night in front of Petersburg. We can see Petersburg from here. There has been some cannonading along the line today but we don't mind that, it is an every day occurrence. Now my dear I will bid you goodnight may God bless and take care of us all till we meet. My love to you and my dear little pets. Your affectionate husband,

J. W. Brendel

Write soon. Tell me in your next all about the draft.

Written to:
Mrs. Ann M. Brendel
West Newton, Westmorland County, Penna.

Ambulance Department
February 22, 1865

My Dear Wife,

I sit down with pleasure to answer your two kind and welcomed letters of the 10th and 16th that came to hand yesterday and today and was very glad to hear that you was as well as can be expected. I hope that God will restore you to good health again. My health is good as usual. I am broke down I am not the same stout John I was three years ago. But I feel very thankful to my heavenly father for his goodness towards me in sparing my life and health through so many dangers which he has brought me through, while thousands have fell by my side and I am still spared and trust in God that he will still continue his goodness towards me and spare me to get home once more. We had two days hard fighting come out victorious held the ground we gain. The 5th Corps are putting up quarters again along the line on the ground we gained. The ambulance department are still in the same quarters. I don't think we will move the train for it takes so much work to put up the stabling. We moved the field hospital out where the troops are quartered. I visited the brigade last Sunday, saw Will he is well. There is talk that we will be paid in a few days. I hope it may be so for I think it is time. As soon as we are paid I will send you some money for I know you need it as bad as I do and a little worse I suppose. You can tell Mrs. Obly that Fred is well and makes a good soldier. I have not saw Andy Neff or any of the rest of the West Newton boys since the battle, only James Brundige, he is well and makes a first rate soldier. My dear wife, you say you got no letters from me since the battle. I wrote you two since the fight and this is the third. I wrote on the 11th as soon as I got back you ought to had it before you wrote the last one to me. Write soon, no more at present only my love to you and my dear little children. May God bless and protect us all until we meet again. Your affectionate husband,

J. W. Brendel
Sergeant Company G., 11th Regiment P.V.

Written to:
No envelope

Ambulance Department Virginia
February 26, 1865

My Dear Annie,

Your kind letter of the 20th came to hand and duly read and was glad to hear that you was all well. I am well but don't feel much like writing. I was on guard last night and did not any sleep and so you will have to excuse the shortness of my letter. Some of the pay masters are here paying part of the Fifth Corps and I think we will be paid or a part at least in a few days we only got four months pay but I hope we will get the whole six months for we stand in need of it. As soon as we are paid I will send you some money and write to you. Brother William is well, the weather is pleasant here warm enough to go in your shirt sleeves. Thunder showers roads very muddy. The Johnnie Rebs are deserting very fast. There is from thirty to two-hundred comes in every day. They come here to the station to take the train for Washington. They appear to think rebellion is gone up the spout. You will have to excuse this scribbled up letter. The next one I will try and do better. No more my dear wife but my sincere to you and the children your affectionate husband.

J. W. Brendel

Write soon

Between February 26 and March 25, approximately 1,800 Confederates deserted. While on picket duty, small groups of Confederates would crawl under the cover of darkness over to the Union lines. One estimate by John S. Preston, Superintendent of the Bureau of Conscription, stated that as of February at least 100,000 Confederates had deserted throughout the Confederacy.[7]

Written to:
Mrs. Ann M. Brendel
West Newton, Westmorland County, Penna.

Ambulance Department Virginia
March 11th 1865

My Dear Annie,

I sit down this evening to answer your long looked for letter of the first of March came to hand today and I was very glad to hear that you was all well. I am pretty well thank God and hope these few lines may find you all enjoying the same blessing. We was paid a part of our money, settled up our clothing till the first of January and paid the balance due us till then. We are looking to be paid off again in a few days. I will send you some money as soon as I can get a chance to express it. I was out on picket with six ambulance wagons and was just relieved today or I would have sent you some money before this. I went to army headquarters before I went on picket but there was no agent. There is none nearer than City Point that is fifteen miles from here. I will get a chance in a day or two to send it and I expect we will be paid in a few days again. I will send thirty dollars now and forty as we are paid. There is forty dollars coming to me now that I am mustered, for besides this month my clothing bill was eighty-three dollars and sixty-five cents since I settled before. Now my dear wife, I think I will close for this time as I have not had much rest for a few days and will write you a long love letter as soon as I get a letter from you. Brother William is home on furlough his furlough will soon be out. I suppose you know it before now. Good night my dear wife, my love to you, kiss my dear little pets for me and tell them to be good children. The weather is warm here but it has been very wet. Good night may God take care of us till we meet. Your affectionate husband,

John W. Brendel

To his faithful Annie, write soon for it appears a long time between letters only two since the 20th of February. I would send you money in this letter but I am afraid you might not get it for the letters come so un-regular and money is too scarce to be lost now.

Written to:
Mrs. Ann M. Brendel
Westnewton, Westmoreland Co. Penna.
*Soldiers Letter

Ambulance Department
March 28, 65

My Dear Wife:

I sit down to drop you a few lines to let you know I am well and hope you are enjoying the same blessing. I received a letter from you dated March the 18th and stated you had not got the money I expressed. I expressed twenty-five dollars to you the 14th and wrote you a letter and sent the receipt. I had allowed to send you seventy dollars if I had got my money but they only settled last years account and I received no wages this year. But I hope they will soon pay off and then I can send you enough money to pay off all your debts and have some left. Enclosed you will find two dollars. You must excuse me for not writing more for I have not time to write. We are busy making plans for the spring campaign. We had a little fight in front of Petersburg last Saturday captured over three thousand Reb prisoners and have been stirring around ever since, have not much time to do anything. The Second and Ninth Corps done the fighting this time. No more at present. My love to you, I hope to get home in August. That is not long anymore. May God bless and spare us too. Your affectionate husband,

John W. Brendel

Write soon for I am anxious to hear from you. Give my love to all inquiring friends.

Until now, the Union lines formed an arc extending from north of Petersburg to southeast of Petersburg. In late March, Grant devised a plan to proceed to the west, thus capturing the South Side Railroad and forcing Lee from Petersburg. The 11th Pennsylvania along with the Fifth Corps was part of this action. The 11th Pennsylvania would leave the entrenchments around Petersburg for good this time. The Confederate line was thinly held in the direction of the Union advance.

After leaving camp at Hatchers Run, the 11th Pennsylvania engaged in a series of battles known as the Five Forks Campaign. This action occurred between March 29 and April 1. On March 29th at the Battle of Lewis' Farm, the Fifth Corps moved up the Quaker Road at the Boydton Plank Road where they encountering Maj. General Bushrod Johnson's Confederates. After a sharp encounter, the Confederates were forced back to their entrenchments on the White Oak Road.

On March 31, Lee shifted troops to meet the Union movements. The Fifth Corps attacked Confederate Entrenchments along White Oak Road. Maj. General Johnson initiated a counter-attack stalling the Fifth Corps. By the end of the day, the Fifth Corps position stabilized and closed on the road.

The Battle of Five Forks was fought on April 1. Five Forks refers to the intersection of the White Oak Road, Scott's Road, Ford's (or Church) Road and the Dinwiddie Court House Road. Lee ordered Maj. General Picket to hold the crossroad at all hazards. The Union attack was led by Maj. General Philip Sheridan. While Sheridan's cavalry pinned down the Confederates, the Fifth Corps attacked and overwhelmed the Confederate left flank. The loss at Five Forks forced Lee to withdraw Confederate forces at Petersburg and Richmond.

After evacuating Petersburg and Richmond, Lee headed west towards Appomattox Station with hopes of moving south to meet up with Maj. General Joseph E. Johnston's army in North Carolina.[8]

The movements of the Fifth Corps in pursuit of Lee passed through Drainsville, crossed the Appomattox River and encamped near Prince Edward's Court House on the night of April 7. The Fifth Corps made a series of long tedious marches over miserable roads. They found evidence of a rapid retreat of the enemy. The Fifth Corps arrived near Appomattox Court House by 9 a.m. on the morning of April 9.[9] According to General Coulter's report "Further movements were now arrested by reception of a truce, which eventuated in the capitulation the same day by the Army of Northern Virginia (Rebel), General Lee to Lieutenant- General Grant.[10]

This is the day that all soldiers look forward to, THE WAR HAS ENDED.

Written to:
Mrs. Ann M. Brendel
Westnewton, Westmoreland Co. Penna.

Ambulance Department, Va.
April 19, 1865

Dear Wife:

I sit down to drop you a few lines to let you know I am living and well and Brother Will is well and hope you are enjoying the same blessing. I received two letters from you since we started on this campaign and had no chance to write to you. But I will write to you as soon as we stop some place. You have all the war news and so I need not tell you about our success since we started on this trip. No more but my love to you my dear. I will write as soon as I can and tell you all the particulars. Write as soon as you get this for I am anxious to hear from you. I am glad you are pleased with your new home. No more may God permit us to meet soon. Your affectionate husband,

J. B. Brendel

Written to:
Mrs. Ann M. Brendel
Westnewton, Westmoreland Co. Penna.

Camp near Washington
May 13th, 1865

Dear Wife:

I received your kind letter this morning and was glad to hear that you was all well. We got here last night after a long and hard march. I think we will get home about the first of June. Now Annie I feel so tired to write much. I think I will just let you know I am well and tell you all about things when I get home. You need not write anymore for I think the Ambulance Corps will be broke up before I would get the letter. I will write to you as soon as we are paid and send you some money. No more my dear love, I will write as soon as I am paid. My love to you and my dear little children. Tell them pap will soon be at home if God spares my health and I hope he will. You wanted to know if I was in Richmond and Petersburg and all the battleground in between Washington and Appomattox Court House where General Lee surrendered. Now I will stop and tell you all about it when I get home. Your affectionate husband,

J. W. Brendel

I expect we will start for Harrisburg in a day or two.

On May 23rd and 24th, just prior to being mustered out, a grand review of Union troops was held in Washington. At least 150,000 troops marched in parade formation as vast crowds of civilians turned out to watch the veterans. People placed garlands of flowers upon the victorious men. The Fifth Corps with Crawford's Third Division was last in line. The Third Brigade, now commanded by Breveted Brig. General Richard Coulter, led the 11 Pennsylvania through the glorious parade. On the reviewing stand were: President Andrew Johnson, Secretary of the Navy Gideon Welles and Generals Grant, Meade and Sherman.[11].

Written to:
Mrs. Ann M. Bendel
Westnewton, Westmoreland Co. Penna.

Camp near Washington D.C.
May 25, 1865

My Dear Annie:

I thought I would drop you a few lines to let you know I am well and hope your enjoying the same blessing. I took four blankets to the Christian Commission today and had them expressed to you. You will have to get them when they come and open them for fear they spoil. I expect to be at home in a few days. They are making out our discharge papers today. I expect to be mustered out tomorrow. I will send you some money as soon as we are paid and I expect I will be at home in about a week. William is well, no more, my love to you and my dear children. I will be home soon if God spares my life and health. Your affectionate husband,

J. W. Brendel

Army Wagons - City Point, Virginia. Possibly ambulance wagons. (LOC)

*Wash Infantry - Washington, D.C.
Infantry unit with fixed bayonets followed by ambulances on Pennsylvania Avenue
near the Treasury at the Grand review of the army, May, 1865. (LOC)*

After the war, Brendel returned home to his family in West Newton. John and Anna added to their family with a son William, born in 1866. Another son, Frank, was born in 1869. As of 1870, John's occupation was still that of a shoe and boot maker.

John W. Brendel survived the war by only seven years. He died on September 23, 1872 of kidney trouble and is buried in the West Newton Cemetery. Anna would survive her husband by forty-three years. In 1912, Anna was denied a pension for her first husband John W. Brendel from the United States Government because she could not prove his death was the result of injuries received during the Civil War. She claimed John's death could be attributed to wounds received at the Battle of Antietam. She was referring to the back injury John sustained at the Battle of South Mountain three days prior to Antietam. However, John's back injury was not documented on the muster-rolls. Even though it was apparent through his letters that his back bothered him throughout the war, without proper documentation Anna was not eligible to receive benefits. Their son Frank applied for a minor's Pension from the date of the death of his father until he turned sixteen but his claim was denied. The government stated that Anna was the only person entitled to submit a claim and her claim was denied.

On September 22, 1881 in West Newton, Anna married another Civil War soldier: Anthony Growall. This was the second marriage for both of them. Growall's first wife Sarah, was tragically killed in a circular rip saw accident at a planing mill on March 19, 1880. Growall Served with the 142nd Pennsylvania Volunteer Infantry, Company C. He joined about the same time as Brendel, serving from August 26, 1862 to July 3, 1865. Growall died on March 15, 1902. Anna received a small pension ranging from six to twelve dollars per month, due to injuries Growall had incurred during the Civil War. Growell suffered from a back injury, deafness and a disease in his left eye. Anna died in 1915 and was buried in West Newton next to her first husband John W. Brendel.

Like thousands of other soldiers, Brendel and his family suffered considerably during the Civil War period. Torn between the nation's troubles and family obligations Brendel managed to remain upbeat. Going from making shoes and boots before the war to shooting at his fellow man during the war had to be a life altering experience. It seems as though his faith in God and family carried him through the darkest of days.

It is our duty to pay homage to the men and women, who faithfully served this country. It is the editor's hope that this book fulfills that responsibility.

Jenny and Anna Brendel with Jenny's son Frank Cooper

Samuel Brendel

Jenny Brendel

Robert Brendel

B 1.

John W. Brindle

Corp., Co. G, 11 Reg't Pa. Infantry.

Age 37 years.

Appears on a
Detachment Muster-out Roll

of the organization named above. Roll dated
Mt. Washington, May 31, 1865.
Muster-out to date   May 31, 1865.
Last paid to   Dec. 31, 1864.

Clothing account:

Last settled _____, 186 ; drawn since $ ____ 100/100
Due soldier $ _____ 100/100 ; due U. S. $ 9 08/100
Am't for cloth'g in kind or money adv'd $ ____ 100/100

Due U. S. for arms, equipments, &c., $ _____ 100/100
Bounty paid, $ ____ 100/100 ; due, $ 100 100/100.

Remarks:

Book mark:

Paxton

(349)   Copyist.

Appendix A

The following letters written by John W. Brendel are not dated:

Written to:
No Envelope

My Dear Wife;

I believe this is the first letter I ever wrote you on Sunday, but you don't see much difference between Sunday and weekday. We have no drill on Sunday but have inspection and dress parade and roll call evening and morning and sometimes a little preaching. But it is small for it's age. There is a preacher with us all the time but he is not much account. He is a Methodist but I did not give the denomination to hurt your feelings. He don't preach often and it is short when he does. You can hear the drums and fifes going from morning till bed time Sunday and everyday.

J. W. Brendel

The sand is flying, you can hardly see.

Written to:
Mrs. Ann M. Brendel
Westnewton, Westmoreland County, Penna.
*Soldiers Letter- Due 3 Cents

Camp 11th Regt. P.V. Virginia

Dear Wife:

I sit down to drop you a few lines to let you know how I am getting along. I am getting along very well but I am not very well nor don't expect I will be in the army. I wrote you two letters since I received yours and sent you my likeness. I did not put my name in with it. I wanted to see whether you would know the old corporal or not. We have had a great time here last week. We have been packed up four times this week and only went out to the picket line and back. We were to march this morning at 3 and one-half o'clock but everything is quiet this morning. This is Sunday, the whole Corps has been moving around this week. We are the First Corps. They say the Sixth Corps is over the river again. I don't know whether it is or not nor no one here can tell what this move means but I suppose we will know in a few days more what it means. We just came in off picket yesterday. Nothing more at present but remain your affectionate husband,

John W. Brendel

Give my love to all inquiring friends and keep the largest portion for yourself. Give my love to Jennie, Sammy and Robby and tell them to be good children till their pappy comes home. I will not write until I receive some word from you.

The following letter was written by John W. Brendel's brother-in-law William McLaughlin. It was included with Brendel's letters. McLaughlin enlisted with the 11th Pennsylvania Volunteer Infantry Regiment Company C on September 9, 1861. He was promoted to sergeant on April 1, 1864, second lieutenant November 1, 1864, first lieutenant December 5, 1864 and commissioned captain June 30, 1865.

Written to:
No envelope

Camp Curtin, Harrisburg
Sept. 15, 1861

Dear Jennie:

I take pleasure in writing to you this morning to inform you that I am well. I received your letter and was glad to hear from you and all the rest. I have not received any answer from father yet. I don't know whether he got my letter or not. I did not think of writing to you till father would answer my letter but as we are going to leave this camp before long I thought I would write and let you know Col. Coulter was here yesterday and he thought we would leave this camp this week. We will go either to Washington or Winchester probably. We will leave this camp on Friday. There was a regiment left this camp for Washington yesterday but I think we will go to Winchester. I wish we would for there is so many at Washington but we will have to go where we are ordered. I got my clothes down to Harrisburg on Friday and the agent said they would start on Saturday. We had them in a box and the boys said they had no money_____ the freight and the freight was not paid. I wrote to David Laughery and told him to lift my sack and pay the freight and father would pay him. I bought John, Frank and Nancy a little book for a present and mother a pipe. Tell mother to use her pipe and not lay it away. I had to stand guard on Sunday night for the first time. I can't tell you how much I thought of home. I was at church on Sunday Freman Gay, W. Welty and I went to class meeting first and then to preaching. Jennie I wish you could hear the choir singing well. I must quit writing for I must go to drill. Tell Johnny to go and pray that God will take care of me and mother. Don't fret that we are going away from this camp but pray that I might get home again. I will write as soon as we get to Winchester or Washington and tell you where to direct your letter. Your brother,

W. H. McLaughlin

Appendix B

The following is a list of the engagements and movements John W. Brendel participated in with the 11th Pennsylvania Volunteer Infantry and the Ambulance Department.

1862

August 22. . . . . . Mustered into service at Harrisburg, Pa

September 8. . . . . . Arrived in Washington D.C.

September 9. . . . . . Joined 11th Pennsylvania Infantry at Silver Spring, Md.

September 6-24. . . . . . Maryland Campaign

September 14. . . . . . Battle of South Mountain

September 17. . . . . . Battle of Antietam

Sept. 18-Oct. 30. . . . . . Duty near Sharpsburg, Md.

Oct. 30-Nov. 19. . . . . . Movement to Falmouth, Va.

December 12-15. . . . . . Battle of Fredericksburg

1863

Jan.- April 27. . . . . . Winter quarters at Falmouth and Belle Plains, Va.

January 20-24. . . . . . "Mud March" Campaign

April 27 - May 6. . . . . . Chancellorsville Campaign

April 29. . . . . . Battle at Fredericksburg, Va.

May 2-6. . . . . . Battle of Chancellorsville

June 11 - July 24. . . . . . Gettysburg Campaign

July 1-3. . . . . . Battle of Gettysburg

July 11. . . . . . Line of battle near Antietam, MD.

August - September......	Camp near Rappahannock Station, Va.
Sept. 15 - Oct. 10......	Duty along the Rapidan River
November 7-8......	Advance to line of the Rappahannock River
Nov. 26 - Dec. 2......	Mine Run Campaign
December......	Camp near Kelly's Ford

1864

January......	Camp near Cedar Mountain, Va.
February 1......	Camp near Culpeper, Va.
Feb. 5 - March 28......	Furlough- returned home to West Newton, Pa.
April......	Camp near Culpeper, Va.
May - June......	Wilderness Campaign
May 5-7......	Battle of the Wilderness
May 8-12......	Battles at Spotsylvania Court House and surrounding Spotsylvania County
May 8......	Battle of Laurel Hill, Va.
May 12......	Assault on the Salient
May 23-26......	Battle of North Anna (River)
May 26-28......	On the line of the Pamunkey River
May 28-31......	Battle of Totopotomoy Creek (Bethesda Church)
June 1-12......	Battle of Cold Harbor
June 13......	Battle at White Oak Swamp
June 16-18......	Assault at Petersburg, Va.
June 16 - April 1865......	Siege of Petersburg, Va.
July 30......	Battle of the Crater (in reserve)

August 18-21 . . . . . . Weldon Railroad

September 19 . . . . . . Reconnaissance toward Dinwiddie Court House

December 7-12 . . . . . . Raid on Weldon Railroad

1865

February 5-7 . . . . . . Battle of Hatchers Run

March 28 - April 9 . . . . . . Appomattox Campaign

March 29 . . . . . . Battle Lewis farm, Gravelly Run

March 31 . . . . . . Battle at White Oak Road

April 1 . . . . . . Battle of Five Forks

April 9 . . . . . . Appomattox Court House, Surrender of General Lee and the Army of Northern Virginia

May 12 . . . . . . Arrived in Washington D. C.

May 23 . . . . . . Grand review parade of the Union army in Washington D.C.

May 31 . . . . . . Brendel mustered out of service

Army of the Potomac Organization

The 11th Pennsylvania was assigned to the following commands during Brendel's tenure:

August 1862 - May 1863 . . . First Corps, Second Division, Third Brigade

May - July 1863 . . . First Corps, Second Division, Second Brigade

July 1 - July 18, 1863 . . . First Corps, Second Division, First Brigade

July 18 - March 1864 . . . First Corps, Second Division, Second Brigade

March - May 1864 . . . Fifth Corps, Second Division, Second Brigade

May 1864 - March 1865 . . . Fifth Corps, Third Division, Second Brigade

March 1865 - July 1865 . . . Fifth Corps, Third Division, Third Brigade NA

End Notes

Introduction

1 - Robertson, James I., *Soldiers Blue & Gray*, Warner Books Inc., New York, 1991

2 - Bates, Samuel P., *History of Pennsylvania Volunteers*, Harrisburg, B. Singerly, State Printer, 1869 & Broadfoot Publications, Wilmington, North Carolina, 1993

Chapter 1

1 - *Camp Curtin Historical Society* (http://www.campcurtin.org/)

2 - Pennsylvania Historical and Museum Commission- Governor Andrew Gregg Curtin

3 - Lord Francis A., *They Fought For The Union*, Bonanza Books, New York, 1960

4 - Dowdey, Clifford and Manarin, Louise H., *The Wartime Papers of R.E. Lee*, VA Civil War Commission, Bramhall House, NY 1961

5 - Hennessy, John, *Return to Bull Run*, New York: Simon & Schuster 1993 Page 403

6 - Murfin, James V. *The Gleam of Bayonets*, New York: Thomas Yoseloff, 1968 Page 345

7 - Wert, Jeffery D., *The Sword of Lincoln* Page 148, Special Order 191

8 - Bates, Samuel P., *History of Pennsylvania Volunteers*, Harrisburg, B. Singerly, State Printer, 1869 & Broadfoot Publications, Wilmington, North Carolina, 1993

9 - O.R, LI, part 1, pp. 140-142 Col. Richard Coulter report

10 - Gannon James P., *Irish Rebels Confederate Tigers: A history of the 6th Louisiana Infantry 1861-1865, Confederate Veteran Magazine* Vol. 5, 1998

11 - Bates, Samuel P., *History of Pennsylvania Volunteers*

12 - Bates, Samuel P., *History of Pennsylvania Volunteers*

13 - Donald, David Herbert, *Lincoln*, New York, Simon & Schuster 1995 Page 389

14 - Bates, Samuel P., *History of Pennsylvania Volunteers*

15 - Warner, Ezra J., *Generals in Blue*, Louisiana State University Press, Baton Rouge & London 1986, Page 26

16 - Wert, Jeffery D., *The Sword of Lincoln*, Page 184

17 - Robertson, James I., *Soldiers Blue & Gray*

18 - Wert, Jeffery D., *The Sword of Lincoln*, Page 204

19 - Lord, Francis A., *They Fought for the Union*

20 - Stouffer Cindy & Cubbison Shirley, *A Colonel, A Flag and A Dog*, Thomas Publications, Gettysburg, Pa. 1998

21 - Lord Francis A., *They Fought for the Union*

Chapter 2

1 - *Funk & Wagnalls, New Encyclopedia*, Vol.9, 1996 page 210

2 - Bates, Samuel P., *History of Pennsylvania Volunteers*

3 - Frye, Dennis E. & Rob Gibson, Gods and Generals, Photographic Companion, Thomas Publications, Gettysburg, Pa., 2003

4 - Frassinito, William A., Antietam, *The Photographic Legacy of America's Bloodiest Day*, Charles Scribner's Sons, New York, 1978

5 - CWSAC Battle Summaries part of VA28, National Park Service, Washington D.C.

6 - Wert, Jeffery D., *The Sword of Lincoln*

7 - Dammann, Dr. Gordon, *Pictorial Encyclopedia of Civil War Medical Instruments and Equipment*, Volume I, Pictorial Histories Publishing Company, Missoula, Montana 1989, Page 44

8 - Robertson, James I, *Soldiers Blue & Gray*

9 - Gayley, Alice J., 11th Pennsylvania Infantry Regiment, (http://www.pa-roots.com)

10 - Robertson, James I, *Soldiers Blue & Gray*

11 - Donald, David Herbert, *Lincoln*

12 - Smithsonian Institute, http://historywired.si.edu

13 - United States Department of Health and Human Services, Center for Disease Control and Prevention

14 - Lord, Francis, *They Fought for the Union*

15 - *Civil War Times Illustrated*, The Battle of Chancellorsville, Gettysburg, Historical Times Inc. 1968

16 - Bates, Samuel P., *History of Pennsylvania Volunteers*

17 - CWSAC Battle Summaries, Chancellorsville

18 - Bates, Samuel P., *History of Pennsylvania Volunteers*

19 - *Battles and Leaders of the Civil War The Tide Shifts Volume III*, Castle, Secaucus Pages 237, 238

20 - Bates, Samuel P., *History of Pennsylvania Volunteers*

21 - Coddington, Edwin W., *The Gettysburg Campaign: A Study in Command*, Simon & Schuster, New York 1997

22 - Coddington, Edwin W., *The Gettysburg Campaign: A Study in Commad*

23 - Bates, Samuel P., *History of Pennsylvania Volunteers*

24 - Wert, Jeffery D. *The Sword of Lincoln*

25 - Bates, Samuel P., *History of Pennsylvania Volunteers*

26 - Martin, David G., *Gettysburg July 1*, Da Capo Press Cambridge, Massachusetts, 2003

27 - Large, George R., *Battle of Gettysburg The Official History by the Gettysburg National Military Park*, Burd Street Press, 1999

28 - Martin, David G., *Gettysburg July 1*, Page 440

29 - Large, George R., *Battle of Gettysburg*

30 - Sears, Stephen W., *Gettysburg*, Houghton Mifflin Company, Boston & New York, Page 485

31 - Bates, Samuel P., *History of Pennsylvania Volunteers*

32 - Bates, Samuel P., *History of Pennsylvania Volunteers*

33 - Wert, Jeffery D., *The Sword of Lincoln*

34 - Eicher, David J., Deploy the Skirmishers, *Civil War Times*, A Primedia Publication, December, 2003

35 - Coddington, Edwin W., *The Gettysburg Campaign*

36 - Smithsonian Institute, http://civilwar.bluegrass.net/PrisonsParoles And POWs

37 - Dammann, Dr. Gordon, *Pictorial Encyclopedia of Civil War Medical Instuments and Equipment*

38 - Woodworth, Steven, *Civil War Times*, The Meaning of Life and Death in the Valley, A Primedia Publication, December 2003

39 - Mine CWSAC Battle Summaries Run

40 - Bates, Samuel P., *History of Pennsylvania Volunteers*

Chapter 3

1 - Bates, Samuel P., *History of Pennsylvania Volunteers*

2 - Bates, Samuel P., *History of Pennsylvania Volunteers*

3 - Grant, U.S., Grant; *Personal Memoirs of U. S. Grant Selected Letters 1839-1865*, Literary Classics of the United States Inc., New York, 1990

4 - Rhea, Gordon C., *The Battle of The Wilderness, May 5-6, 1864*, Louisiana State University Press, Baron Rouge & London, 1994

5 - Grant, U. S., Grant

6 - Davis, William C., *The Fighting Men of the Civil War*, Salamander Books Limited, London, 1999 re-printed

7 - Rhea, Gordon C., *The Battle of the Wilderness*

8 - Warner Ezra J., *Generals in Blue*

9 - Bates, Samuel P., *History of Pennsylvania Volunteers*

10 - CWSAC, *Battle Summaries*, Spotsylvania

11 - Wert, Jeffery D., *The Sword of Lincoln*

12 - Grant, U.S, *Grant*

13 - Cullen, Joseph P., *The Siege of Petersburg*, Eastern Acorn Press, 1981

14 - McPherson, James M., *Ordeal By Fire*, McGraw-Hill Publication Company, New York, 1982

15 - Cullen, Joseph P., *The Siege of Petersburg*

16 - Smithsonian Institute, http://civilwar.bluegrass.net/battles-campaigns

17 - Cullen, Joseph P., *The Siege of Petersburg*

18 - Bates, Samuel P., *History of Pennsylvania Volunteers*

19 - National Park Service, *Petersburg National Battlefield Map & Guide*

20 - Donald, David Herbert, *Lincoln*

21 - Donald, David Herbert, *Lincoln*

22 - DeGregoria, William A., *The complete Book Of U.S. Presidents*, Wings Books, New York, 1986

23 - CWSAC, Battle Summaries, *Boydton Plank Road*

24 - Warner, Ezra J., *Generals in Blue*

25 - National Park Service, *Petersburg National Battlefield Map & Guide*

26 - Bates, Samuel P., *History of Pennsylvania Volunteers*

27 - http://americancivilwar.com/sanitary

28 - Dowdey, Clifford and Manarin, Louis H., *The Wartime Papers of R.E.Lee*, Virginia, Civil War Commission, Bramhall House, New York 1961

29 - Newman & Eisenschiml, *The Civil War An American Iliad*, The Blue & Gray Press 1985

Chapter 4

1 - The National Historical Society, *The Image of War*, Volume IV, Fighting for Time

2 - Munson, Edward L. M.D, *Photographic History of the Civil War*, Volume IV, The Blue & Gray Press, New Jersey 1987

3 - Official Records of the War of the Rebellion, General Order No. 147

4 - Munson, Edward L. M.D., *Photographic History of the Civil War*

5 - Cullen, Joseph P., *The Siege of Petersburg*

6 - Bates, Samuel P., *History of Pennsylvania Volunteers*

7 - Wiley, Bell Irvin, *The Life of Johnny Reb, The Common Soldier of the Confederacy*, The Louisiana University Press, Baton Rouge & London 1988

8 - CWSAC, Battle Summaries, Battle of Lewis's Farm, Battle of White Oak Road & Battle of Five Forks

9 - Bates, Samuel P., *History of Pennsylvania Volunteers*

10 - O.R. Vol. XLVI, PT 1, Coulters Report

11 - Stouffer Cindy and Cubbison, Shirley, *A Colonel, A Flag and a Dog*

Bibliography

Battles and Leaders of the Civil War The Tide Shifts Volume I, II, III, IV, Castle, Secaucus

Bates, Samuel P., *History of Pennsylvania Volunteers*, B. Singerly, State Printer, 1869 & Broadfoot Publications, Wilmington, North Carolina, 1993

Davis, William C., *The Fighting Men of the Civil War*, Salamander Books Limited, London, 1999 re-printed

DeGregorio, William A., *The complete Book Of Presidents*, Wings Books, New York, 1986

Dowdey, Clifford and Manarin, Louis H., *The Wartime Papers of R.E. Lee*, Virginia Civil War Commission, Bramhall House, New York 1961

Camp Curtin Historical Society (http://www.camp curtin.org.)

Civil War times Illustrated, The Battle of Chancellorsville, Gettysburg, Historical Times Inc. 1968 & Deploy the Skirmishers, December 2003

Coddington, Edwin W., *The Gettysburg Campaign: A Study in Command*, Simon & Schuster, New York 1997

Cullen, Joseph P., *The Siege of Petersburg*, Eastern Acorn Press, 1981

CWSAC Battle Summaries part of VA28, National Park Service, Washington D.C.

Dammann, Dr. Gordon, *Pictorial Encyclopedia of Civil War Medical Instruments and Equipment*, Volume I, Pictorial Histories Publishing Company, Missoula, Montana 1989

Donald, David Herbert, *Lincoln*, New York, Simon & Schuster 1995

Frassanito, William A., *Antietam, The Photographic Legacy of America's Bloodiest Days*, Charles Scribner's Sons, New York, 1978

Frye, Dennis E. & Rob Gibson, *Gods and Generals, Photographic Companion*, Thomas Publications, Gettysburg, Pa., 2003

Funk & Wagnalls, *New Encyclopedia*, Vol.9, 1996

Gannon, James P., *Irish Rebels Confederate Tigers: A History of the 6th Louisiana Infantry*, 1861-1865, Confederate Veteran, Vol. 5, 1998

Gayley, Alice J. *11th Pennsylvania Infantry Regiment*, (http://www.pa-roots.com.)

Grant, U. S., Grant; *Personal Memoirs of U. S. Grant Selected Letters 1839-1865*, Literary Classics of the United States Inc., New York, 1990

Hennessy, John, *Return to Bull Run*, New York: Simon & Schuster 1993

Large, George R., *Battle of Gettysburg, The Official History by the Gettysburg National Military Park*, Burd Street Press, 1999

Lord, Francis A., *They Fought For The Union*, Bonanza Books, New York, 1960

Martin, David G., *Gettysburg*, July 1, Page 440

McPherson, James M., *Ordeal By Fire*, McGraw-Hill Publishing Company, New York, 1982

Munson, Edward L. M.D., *Photographic History of the Civil War, Volume IV*, The Blue & Gray Press, New Jersey, 1987

Murfin, James V., *Gleam of Bayonets*, New York, Thomas Yoseloff, 1968

National Park Service, *Petersburg National Battlefield Map and Guide*

Newman & Eisenschiml, *The Civil War An American Iliad*, The Blue & Gray Press 1985

Official Records of the War of the Rebellion

Pennsylvania Historical and Museum Commission - Governor Andrew Gregg Curtin

Pennsylvania Historical and Museum Commission, Pennsylvania Governors Past to Present, Governor Andrew Gregg Curtin (http://www.phmc.state.pa.us)

Rhea, Gordon C., *The Battle of the Wilderness*, May 5-6, 1864, Louisiana State University Press, Baton Rouge & London, 1994

Robertson, James I, *Soldiers Blue & Gray*, Warner Books Inc. New York, 1991

Sears, Stephen W., *Landscape Turned Red & Gettysburg*, New Haven & New York, Ticknor & Fields, 1983

Smithsonian Institute, (http://historywired.si.edu) & (http://bluegrass.net/battles-campaigns)

Stouffer, Cindy & Cubbison, Shirley, *A Colonel, A Flag and A Dog*, Thomas Publications, Gettysburg, Pa. 1998

The National Historical Society, *The Images of War*, Volume IV, Fighting for Time

United States Department of Health and Human Services, Center for Disease Control and Prevention, Smallpox Overview (http://www.hhs.gov/smallpox)

Warner, Ezra J., *Generals in Blue*, Louisiana State University, Baton Rouge & London, 1986

Warren, H. N. Col., *War History 1861-1865 (142nd Pennsylvania Volunteer Infantry)*, The Courier Company Printers, Buffalo, New York, 1890

Wert, Jeffery D., *The Sword of Lincoln*, New York: Simon & Schuster 2005

Wiley, Bell Irvin, *The Life of Johnny Reb; The Common Soldier of the Confederacy*, The Louisiana University Press, Baton Rouge & London 1988

Index

A

Adams Express- 8, 12, 13, 74
Alexandria Va.- 89, 90, 91
Allegheny County, Md.-12, 26, 33, 37, 38
Anderson, William- 43
Annapolis Md.- 69
Antietam (battle of)- 17, 18, 21, 22, 31, 36, 47, 51, 63, 66, 86,
Antietam Creek, Md.- 17, 22
Appomattox Court House, Va.- 7, 160, 161
Aquia Creek Va.- 26, 27
Army of Northern Virginia- 13, 98, 160
Army of the Potomac- 8, 9, 49, 56, 67, 80
Army of Virginia- 13
Ausburn Dr., -103

B

Baltimore, Md.- 15, 33, 61
Barnesville, Md.-58
Bates, Edward U.S. Attorney General- 48
Baxter's Brigade- 59
Baxter, Henry, Brigadier-General- 58, 59, 90, 95
Bayard, George, Brigadier-General- 23
Bealeton Station, Va.- 24, 74, 75, 79
Belle Isle Prison, Va.- 68
Belle Plain Landing, Va.- 27, 28, 32, 33, 34, 36,-39, 41- 45, 49, 50, 66
Belle Vernon, Pa.- 42, 73
Berlin (Brunswick) Md. 22, 63
Bermuda Hundred, Va.- 119
Bierer, Jacob, Captain- 14, 18, 19
Bloody Angle (Spotsylvania Court House, Va, battle of)- 96

Boonsboro, Md.- 16

Boydton Plank Road- 117, 159

Braddock Road (old) - 16

Brendel, Ell (sister of John W. Brendel)- 24, 75, 96, 102

Brendel, Frank- 164, 165

Brendel, Jacob (brother of John W. Brendel)- 45, 70, 73, 75, 116, 147

Brendel, Jenny- 7, 21, 26, 28, 32, 35- 40, 43, 45, 51, 54, 55, 74, 75, 81, 83, 93, 102, 103, 105, 108, 111, 114-116, 120, 123, 127, 129, 131, 132, 135, 136, 139, 142, 145, 165, 168

Brendel, Liz- 43

Brendel, Lucy (married to Jacob Brendel)- 45

Brendel, Robert (Robby)- 7, 26, 28, 36, 37, 43, 45, 54, 55, 74, 75, 82, 102, 103, 106, 111,112, 114, 116, 129, 131, 132, 135, 136, 139, 142, 145, 165, 168

Brendel, Samuel- 7, 43, 45, 51,52, 55, 93, 111, 116, 120, 123, 152, 165, 168

Brendel, William- 164,

Brindle, Martha- 46

Bristoe Station, Va.- 78

Brundige, James- 155

Bull Run, battle of- 13-15, 42, 68

Burkhart, Davie, 151

Burnside, Ambrose, Major General- 22, 23, 35, 36, 94

Butler, Benjamin, Major General-118,119

C

Camp Curtin (Harrisburg, Pa.)- 11, 12, 15, 20, 72, 169

Carlisle, Pa.- 68

Catoctin Mountains, Md.- 61

Cedar Mountain, Va.- 85, 87, 88

Centreville, Va.- 58

Chancellorsville, Va.- 53, 83, 95

Chancellorsville, battle of- 95

City Point, Va.- 103, 104, 132, 133, 134, 136- 141, 143, 157, 163

Clothing (uniform)- 66, 166

Coal Valley, Pa.- 6, 7

Cold Harbor, Va.- 97, 98

Cooper, Frank- 165
Corbin's Bridge, Va. (Spotsylvania Court House, battle of)- 96
Coulter, Richard, Colonel- 15, 17, 58, 62, 95, 160, 169
Crampton's Gap-16
Crater, battle of- 101
Culpeper, Va.- 57, 64, 75, 88, 91-94
Cupping (medical procedure)- 73, 74, 102
Curry, George- 86
Curtin, Andrew, Governor of Pennsylvania- 11

D

Davis, Jefferson, President Confederate States of America- 13
Doubleday, Abner, Brigadier General- 58
Dranesville, Va.- 13
Dysentery- 40

E

Early, Jubal, Lieutenant- General-105
Edwards Ferry, Va.- 58
Election, presidential, 1864- 113,114
Emmittsburg, Md.- 58
Ewell, Richard, Lieutenant-General- 105
Ewell's, Richard, Corps- 57

F

Falmouth, Va.- 83
Five Forks, Va.- 159, 160
Fletchers Chapel- 49, 52
Fort Dushane, Va.- 110-113, 115, 116
Fort Wadsworth, Va.- 116, 117, 119, 120, 123-125, 128-131
Fourth United States Artillery Battery B- 59
Fox, Gust- 67, 69
Fox, William- 69
Fox's Gap- 16
Frederick, Md.- 61, 62
Fredericksburg, Va.- 23, 42, 47, 53, 54, 56, 57, 69, 83
Frithman, Irvin- 37, 69

Funkstown, Md.- 62

G

Gay, Freman- 169
Gettysburg, battle of- 9, 29, 30, 39, 58-64, 67, 69, 78, 83, 86, 100
Gettysburg National Cemetery- 80
Grant, U.S., Lieutenant- General- 90, 92, 96- 98
Greenfield, Ill.- 115
Greensburg, Pa.- 90
Gregg, John- 52
Growall, Anthony- 164
Growall, Sarah- 164
Guilford Station, Va.- 58

H

Hagerstown, Md.- 16, 61
Halleck, Henry W., Major-General- 58, 96
Hancock, Winfield Scott, Major General- 90, 117
Hanks, John- 113
Harpers Ferry, 16, 20, 22, 58
Harrisburg, Pa.- 11, 12, 14, 21, 26, 33, 66, 70, 86, 90, 91, 161, 169
Harris Farm, (Spotsylvania Court House, battle of)- 96
Harrison House, (Spotsylvania Court House, battle of)- 96
Hartsuff, George, Brigadier- General- 17
Hatchers Run, battle of- 29, 159
Haversack- 51
Hays, Harry, Brigadier-General- 17
Hays, Mont- 44, 45, 67
Herndon, Va.- 58
Heth, Harry, Major-General- 105
Hewitt Mary- 46
Hill, Daniel Harvey, Division- 16
Hoke, Bent, 116, 151
Hooker, Joseph, Major-General- 36, 42, 48, 52, 53, 58

I

Iverson's Brigade- 59

J

Jackson T.J (Stonewall) Lieutenant-General- 16, 28, 54

James River, Va.- 68, 104

Jericho Mills, Va.- 97

Jersey Shore, Pa.- 90

Jerusalem Plank Road- 141, 145, 146

Johnson, Andrew, President of The United States- 162

Johnson, Bushrod, Major–General- 159

Johnston, Joseph, General-160

K

Keedysville, Md.- 63

Kelly's Ford, Va.- 80-82

Koontz, Croft- 15

L

Lake Erie- 129

Latrobe, Pa.- 14

Laughery, David- 169

Laurel Hill, battle of- 96

Lee, Robert E., General- 13, 16, 61, 68, 92, 97, 105, 142, 153, 159, 160, 161

Letterman, Jonathan, Medical Director- 149

Lewis Farm, battle of- 159

Lighty Mr.- 37, 38, 41, 45, 99, 102-104, 107, 112, 114, 118

Lincoln, Abraham, President of The United States- 9, 13, 22, 31, 36, 47, 48, 80, 113

Lincoln, Mary- 48

Locke, William, Regimental Chaplain 11th Pa. Infantry- 59

Lock Haven, Pa.- 90

Logan, William- 41

Longstreet, James, Lieutenant-General- 16

Louisiana, 6th Infantry Regiment- 17

M

Martinsburg, Va.- 16

Mason/Dixon Line- 58

Massachusetts, 12th Infantry Regiment- 17, 18, 70
   13th Infantry Regiment- 17
   39th Infantry Regiment- 153

Mauch Chunk Pa.- 90

McClellan, George B. Major-General- 9, 13, 15, 20-22, 112, 114, 149

McGrew, John, Captain- 7, 15, 28, 33, 34

McLaughlin, Lawyer- 15, 20, 25, 36, 38, 39, 41, 43, 44, 48, 77, 78, 100

McLaughlin, William- 15, 19, 20, 25, 41, 43, 44, 48, 77, 78, 86, 100, 116, 117, 120, 123, 130, 147, 151, 153, 154, 156, 160, 168, 169

Meade, George G, Major-General- 16, 24, 58, 61, 62, 68, 80, 90, 92, 162

Middleburg, Va.- 63, 64

Middletown, Md.- 58

Mine Run Expedition- 80

Moreford, Ida- 122

N

Neff, Andy- 67, 116, 155

Neff, John, 69

Neff, Manuel, 69

New York, 9th Infantry Regiment- 70
   83rd Infantry Regiment- 17
   97th Infantry Regiment- 70

New York Lottery- 82

Newton, John, Major-General- 58

North Anna River, Va.- 96, 97

Ny River, (Spotsylvania Court House, Battle of)- 96

O

Oglesby, Richard- 113

O'Neal's Alabama troops- 59

Orange & Alexandria Railroad- 65

Overly, Fred- 147, 155

P

Pennsylvania, 11th Cavalry Regiment- 34, 36, 129
   11th Infantry Regiment- 7-9, 14-17, 19, 28, 29, 31, 36, 53, 55, 58, 59, 62, 63, 80, 89, 90, 95, 96, 105, 153, 159, 162, 168
   48th Infantry Regiment- 101
   84th Infantry Regiment- 41, 42

136th Infantry Regiment- 56
  142nd Infantry Regiment- 164
Penny, R.- 116
Petersburg, Va.- 98, 99 100, 102-105, 108-110, 111, 121, 133, 142, 152, 154, 158-161
Pittsburg Bank- 15, 19
Pittsburg, Pa.- 12, 34, 46-48, 90, 91, 94, 136
Plummer, George- 22, 28, 46, 90, 95, 98, 102, 103, 107, 114, 132, 138
Pope, John, Major-General- 13
Po River, Va. (Spotsylvania Court House, battle of)- 96
Potomac River, Md.- 13, 22, 46, 58, 61
Preston, John S., Superintendant of the Bureau of Conscription- 157
Prince Edward's Courthouse- 160

Q
Quaker Road, Va.- 159

R
Rappahannock Station, Va.- 65- 67, 69, 71, 72, 74
Rappahannock River, Va.- 23, 35, 45, 46, 52, 53, 55, 64, 73, 75, 80
Rapidan River, Va.- 75, 77, 78, 80
Reed, Francis- 39
Reynolds, John, Major-General- 58
Richmond, Va.- 26, 68, 69, 92, 97, 98, 118, 126, 160, 161
Robinson, John C. Brigadier-General- 90
Rodes, Robert, Brigadier-General- 16
Ross, Jacob (brother-in-law of John W. Brendel)- 93, 96

S
Savannah, Ga.- 142
Sedgwick, John, Major-General- 90
Shaffer, Sarah- 94, 142
Sharpsburg, Md.- 16, 17, 20, 21, 26
Shepherdstown, Va.- 57
Shepler, John- 45, 46
Sheridan, Philip, Major-General- 142, 159
Sherman, William T., Major-General- 142, 162
Sikes, Tom- 146

Silver Spring, Md.- 15
Smallpox- 50
South Mountain, (battle of)- 7, 16, 18-22, 26, 42, 43, 47, 62, 65, 164
Southside Railroad, Va.- 117, 130, 137, 159
Spotsylvania Court House, Va.- 96
Steele, James- 135, 136

T

Thoroughfare Gap, Va.- 77, 78
Twitchell, Elizabeth (sister of John W. Brendel)- 115, 116, 127, 152
Turner's Gap-16

U

United States Christian Commission- 100, 128, 133, 137- 139, 162
United States Sanitary Commission- 134, 139

W

Wadsworth's Brigade- 95
Wadsworth, James, Major-General- 120
Warren, Gouverneur, Major General- 90, 108
Warren's Fifth Corps- 105
Warrenton Va.- 21, 23, 58, 64
Washington County, Md.- 20
Washington City (DC)- 12-14, 20, 28, 33, 39, 57, 58, 61, 65, 77, 86, 87, 89-92, 156, 161-163, 169
Weldon City, NC- 132, 133
Weldon Railroad, Va.- 105-108, 110, 121, 133, 151
Wells, Gideon, Secretary of the Navy- 162
Welty, W.- 169
Werrick, Ios- 102
Westmoreland County, Pa- 7, 14
White Oak Road, Va.- 159
Williamsport Md. 57, 61, 63
Winchester, Va.- 169
Winchester Turnpike- 22
Wisconsin, 8th & 12th Infantry Regiments- 29
Wolford farm- 58

About The Editor

Justin T. Mayhue is a life long resident of Hagerstown, Maryland and serves as a battalion chief for the Hagerstown Fire Department. Mr. Mayhue also teaches firefighting related classes with the Maryland Fire & Rescue Institue, University of Maryland.

Mr. Mayhue possesses an avid interest in Civil war History. Mr. Mayhue serves as a battlefield guide at the Antietam National Battlefield and president of the Hagerstown Civil War Roundtable.

Mr. Mayhue has written four other books including;

"Valor: The Story of PFC Clyde Jacob Smith" (Korea), Printed by Hagerstown Bookbinding & Printing-1998

"Through The Eyes of Fire", Printed by Phoenix Color-1999

"Firefighting in Hagerstown" Arcadia Publications, South Carolina-2004

"Hagerstown Firefighting Through The Years Arcadia publications, South Carolina-2005